Leading Causes of
LIFE

FIVE FUNDAMENTALS TO CHANGE THE WAY YOU LIVE YOUR LIFE

Gary Gunderson

with

Larry Pray

ABINGDON PRESS
Nashville

LEADING CAUSES OF LIFE™
FIVE FUNDAMENTALS TO CHANGE THE WAY YOU LIVE YOUR LIFE

This book is printed on acid-free paper.

Library of Congress Cataloging-in-Publication Data

Gunderson, Gary.
 Leading causes of life / Gary Gunderson with Larry Pray. — Rev. ed.
 p. cm.
 Includes bibliographical references.
 ISBN 978-0-687-65533-5 (binding:/trade pbk., adhesive perfect : alk. paper)
 1. Life. I. Pray, Larry. II. Title.

 BD431.G845 2009
 248.4—dc22

                              2008032547

09 10 11 12 13 14 15 16 17 18—10 9 8 7 6 5 4 3 2 1
MANUFACTURED IN THE UNITED STATES OF AMERICA

Contents

Foreword 7

Introduction: Life Speaks 9

1. Choose Life 19

2. What's a Cause? 43

3. Connection 65

4. Coherence 87

5. Agency 103

6. Blessing 119

7. Hope 129

8. Life Together 141

9. Let Your Life Be About Life 161

Endnotes 187

I have set before you life and death, blessings and cursings;
therefore, choose life,
that both you and your descendants
may live.

DEUTERONOMY 30:19b

I have come that they might
have life,
and have it to the full.

JOHN 10:10b, NIV

Why do you seek the living
among the dead?

LUKE 24:5b

FOREWORD

I have chased death around the world. Famine in Africa, civil war in Central America. Tsunami, hurricane, earthquake. But I wasn't searching for death in these places—I was looking for life and writing about how life prevails in the midst of death-dealing circumstances. But as Gary Gunderson and Larry Pray state in their book, *Leading Causes of Life*, you won't find life by staring at death.

Often life is quiet, courageous, and heroic. Death is sometimes explosive, crushing, and cataclysmic. It comes crashing in when a shell explodes in a village. It comes with the thunderous winds of hurricanes. We've seen and heard far too much of death lately, and we've talked about life less than we should.

We often frame such events by how many people have died, or what those who suffer lack; because this is how we try to grasp the scope of circumstances. However, this framing can desensitize us to deep suffering and leave us emotionally bereft. It can make problems seem too big to resolve. And it's just plain depressing. Death does not lead to life.

I reflected on these thoughts as I read Gunderson and Pray. The roots of life, they write, are to be found in coherence, connection, agency (action), blessing, and hope. These five create the environment in which we can flourish regardless of the diseases, pathologies, or deficits we experience. And they empower us in ways that strengthen whole communities even as they empower individuals.

This has very practical value for me. I find myself involved these days in discussions about why I believe we should end malaria and whether this is too visionary to be accomplished. These conversations are with people who are genuinely concerned about others and are mature in their religious faith: "If we emphasize ending malaria I'm afraid we will de-emphasize HIV/AIDS," writes one. "If we start saving all these lives, as horrible as it is to think about, won't we contribute to the over-population problem?" asks another.

When we isolate problems and focus on deficits, we put causes into competition with each other, write Gunderson and Pray. Our vision is constricted by the limits that we believe bind us. They don't recommend simple positive thinking, however. They say we must look deeply at causes and effects. We must confront death-dealing conditions realistically. When we do this, we find that malaria and HIV/AIDS, for example, need not compete for money and attention. They are interrelated and affect the whole human family. We are connected, as are the circumstances of these deadly diseases. They flourish where poverty exists.

Rather than focus on death, we need strategies for life—empowering individuals and communities by encouraging discussion and solving problems, creating economic opportunities so that all have opportunity to thrive, creating health systems that are accessible and affordable for everyone, providing information about basic sanitation, contagion, clean water, and disease prevention. These strategies integrate disparate causes and unify us around holistic solutions that give us life. They foster coherence, not competition.

I often hear what can't be done, and how limited resources are. This is what happens when we focus on what we lack and pull inward because of fear. Gunderson and Pray remind us that in a world of great abundance and equally great creativity and skill, to believe that we cannot change the death-dealing circumstances that crush vulnerable people, and to repeat that we don't have resources to do justice is merely repeating a litany of death.

Life is present in every community; and the challenge life presents to us is to find it, grab hold, and run with it because life is moving on. We have a choice, of course. Life or death. Gunderson and Pray tell us the language of death is easy to speak, but they call us to make a different choice and find a new language. They remind us the more we speak of death, the more we forget about life. And they ask, "Why not look for the causes of life?" Indeed, why not?

Larry Hollon
General Secretary of United Methodist Communications

INTRODUCTION
Life Speaks

Life has a language. If we are to find our lives on this violent, troubled planet, we must learn the language of life. Then we can tune our ears to it so that we can choose life instead of death. It is there to hear once we know what to listen for—even when we least expect it.

I see two faces and one hope that need a common language of life.

Mike Heidingsfield is a cop right out of central casting: blond, intense, even his sunglasses look right. Now head of the Memphis Crime Commission, intelligence and passion flow off him like heat waves from a Baghdad parking lot. But like his counterparts in all major cities in the U.S., he is near despair about how to reverse the rise of violent crime and its paralyzing grip. The language of death is clear. It tells of unwed mothers and the broken relationships that cycle through loss of respect and revenge again and again. The language of death illuminates the new economy and the missing rungs on the economic ladder that leave little hope. It helps us describe the erosion of local governmental capacity as law enforcement funds flow toward "homeland security" and its distant ghosts. The language helps us describe super predators and repeat victims. Mike looks at me and asks, "Do you really think there is anything about this that we don't know?"

Well, no. I have little to add to the description of death and its causes. But if you're looking for life amid the 16,000 homicides a year, yes, there are certainly some things we are missing. And they'll stay missing until we find another language, the language of life. That's the only thing that helps us understand somebody like TJ.

TJ claims to be two years and nine months old, although his 240 very energetic pounds give us a clue that he is counting from his second birth, not the first one about 20 years earlier. He is the face of everything we fear and hope for when we talk about violence, race, and faith. The "three-year-old" TJ is pastor of the Greater Fellowship Faith Tabernacle Full Gospel Baptist Church. The older TJ was a violent, drug-running gangster known for his dead eyes and heart of stone. Crackling brilliant, charismatic, and passionate, he became a multi-national player at 15, a master of the streets. When his brother Durrell was murdered, he prepared to find and kill seven men in the cycle of revenge that Mike Heidingsfield would regard as predictable as nightfall.

Inexplicably that cycle did not roll through another seven lives. TJ found life instead. And then he found a shared life with a new wife and a life-giving vocation through the saving intervention of Bishop William Young, whom you will meet later in the book. Today TJ has a voice that cuts like a flame through the despair of the streets and carries him across the nation into hundreds of young lives who have known only death.

You need a whole new language to talk about TJ—a language of life. The basic grammar of life is found here: the connection through which life came even in his near total isolation, the coherence of God's grace against the chaos of loss, the sense of agency that could harness such powerful intelligence and energy, the nearly forgotten blessing that flows to TJ from his great-grandparents and through him to hundreds of children, and a hope powerful enough to burn in what was a very dark heart.

> **You can hear how life is speaking—and has spoken—to you using the vocabulary of its five causes: connection, coherence, agency, blessing, and hope.**

The old TJ died. But what caused the new one to explode into such vitality? The story of TJ is about reversal and redemption for which the language of violence and death has no words at all. But life does.

If we can learn life's language, we can see it, work with it, and maybe even more deeply discover our own life in the process. To walk the streets these days you'd better understand Mike's language or you'll be living in a hopelessly naïve bubble. But if you can't talk about TJ's life, you're just as naïve about what's going on around you.

Life has a language and the Leading Causes of Life are a guide to its core structure. Every human being should be able to name the parts of speech, underline the verbs, listen to its nuances, and trace the way it shapes the stories of our lives. As you read you may reflect on your own life language, your vocation, your community, and the institutions to which you relate. You can hear how life is speaking—and has spoken—to you using the vocabulary of its five causes: connection, coherence, agency, blessing, and hope. Although at first glance they seem so easy to define, they actually call for a careful and painstaking definition.

We write about **connection**, grounding that word not just in the social milieu, but in the world of ideas and the healing presence of mountains, rivers, and roads as well.

> Hope does not escape circumstance, it transcends it.

We write about **hope** to release that word from wishful thinking. Hope does not escape circumstance, it transcends it.

We write about **blessing** to encounter its power when we look beyond the gentle tones of "God bless you." Blessing is not the end but the beginning of a conversation with life.

We write about **coherence** to name our relentless desire for belonging, our search for an authentic voice in each of our lives, and the discipline its power can be used for life or death, depending on the choices we make.

We write about **agency** to reclaim it from its institutional use. Say "agency" and most of us think of government. When we write about agency we recognize it as the capacity to act, the fact of change that happens, happens again, and then keeps on happening in all of our lives.

> Blessing is not the end but the beginning of a conversation with life.

Definition, of course, requires the voice of experience. Larry and I couldn't help but trace the stories of our lives as we wrote about each of the five Leading Causes of Life. You too can frame the Leading Causes of Life through the lens of your own experience. Larry's vision of our Leading Causes of Life is framed in part by his experience as a pastor in a no-stoplight Montana town. For Larry, Sunday mornings provide an opportunity to regain a measure of fluency in the language of life. My view on the causes is framed by my work as an executive at a large health system in Memphis as well as by my work in Africa with friends working on AIDS.

The five Leading Causes of Life identified in this book—connection, coherence, agency, blessing, and hope—compel us to write and act.

This book is intended to be useful and portable, like a naturalist's guidebook on trees that is light and compact enough to stick in a pocket. Instead of an arborist's vocabulary of bark, leaves, and soil, we have the five Leading Causes of Life: connection, coherence, agency, blessing, and hope. A guidebook is useful in that it is practical.

As I head out into the neighborhood with my dog, Henry, he knows that such a walk is not a work of science or deep theology. But even on a two-mile lap through the woods, I need some help appreciating the gifts along the way. I need to know what to look for before I can truly understand what I'm seeing. There is a time for the big books left at home on the shelf, just as there is a time for academic conferences about the Leading Causes of Life and retreats to delve into the quiet heart of the God of life. This handbook reminds me to notice what is going on, to look for the detailed fabric of community, and to feel myself as alive, too.

—⁓—

Who should read this book? It is a harder question to answer than it might seem at first.

Any author who thinks that they are writing for somebody else is simply out of touch. You'll see throughout that I'm writing to satisfy my own curiosity about life: about how to be a parent, a friend, a neighbor, a Christian, an administrator; in short, a grown-up. I want to grow up into the service of life and not just back through my years beating away one fear, problem, sickness, or risk after another. I am writing so that my own life can be about life. And I hope you'll find this useful in yours, too.

Then again who would not want to know the causes of life? Who wouldn't want to be fluent in its language? What adult with children and a family, living in a neighborhood, participating in a worshiping community, trying to do useful, lasting work would not want to understand the causes of all that life? For that matter, what adolescents, breaking away from their old confined identities as children, would not want to know how to align their powerful independent vitality with the underlying causes of life? On the other end, what older persons, reflecting on the fruits and losses of their years, would not want to understand what caused their most vital contributions to those that matter most, and maybe how they can continue to be a blessing? Which of us in any positions of leadership of a business, a church, a hospital or any caring institution would not want to consider how we could focus on the causes of life instead of just chasing death into futility? What academic in any discipline would not be intrigued by the opportunity to think about how their work could contribute to life and have a way to think across the boundaries that usually divide us from each others' best insights?

It turns out that life has a language that allows us to talk to each other—deeply and practically—across many barriers that usually divide us. Of course, everyone writing and reading about life has a stake in the subject. I'm talking about the life of the whole neighborhood and the whole community where we find our own lives. The key is changing the focus of conversation from death to life. That's huge. That's the point and is hopefully enough to give us all some hope (and connection, coherence, agency, and blessing, of course).

> **The key is changing the focus of conversation from death to life. That's huge.**

—⁂—

I live in Memphis, Tennessee, where you'd have to be dumb as a box of rocks not to notice the struggle, violence, and brokenness that scatter hope like dry leaves. I help run a hospital that sees 3,000 patients almost every day. Larry lives in Big Timber, Montana, where the scenery is different in every way, but the signals of human struggle are identical. His wife and four kids engage in life despite pain from a rare and chronic genetic disease. Despite two strokes and heart attacks, he continues to engage in ministry that draws its essence from the same river of hope that flows in Memphis.

The two of us listen to the same news you do, so we hear that the high mountain glaciers will melt, the oaks will die, the rivers will run dry, and the cancers will spread. We don't write about life because we live on the cozy, cheerful side. We write because it is too easy to be persuaded that death is winning; that the best we can hope for is to protect ourselves and those we most care for against its inevitable cold grip. It is way too early to say this because life is still going on. And the causes of life are powerful and smart. It is foolish to take them lightly and give in to death so quickly. However many years we may have, we want them to be about life not death; and we hope you do, too.

Once you know where to look, you see life in the most surprising places. There are raccoons and coyotes in downtown Memphis these days. A gaggle of geese, which should be on their way to Canada, have settled on a pond a half-mile from the train yards near my house in Memphis. No buffalo or bear have yet migrated to islands in the Mississippi River, but don't count out life just yet.

There are surprises among humans, too. Amid the transient wreckage of the poverty crescent that loops through the urban core of Memphis, finding a kid with a future seems less likely than finding a buffalo. But you do find them if you know what to look for. You look for life and a glimmer of any of its causes. You look for connection and sense its presence at the coffee shop or office; you look for coherence and notice its power to overcome despair and chaos. You look for agency and are newly aware of all that life is doing and what people are doing as they affirm it. You look for the signs of blessing in changed lives and encouraging words that have the power to frame change. You look for hope and begin to notice its power to transcend circumstance. In short, you'll find enough to say, "I want to be part of it; I want my life to be about life."

In looking for the Leading Causes of Life you probably won't feel naïve or delusional. You may feel like you've noticed something vital, powerful, and compelling. You may feel yourself more connected and sensible. You'll probably sense the possibility of your handful of years being useful for something larger than the economy. You may sense the stirring of choices that matter. You can feel hope, and that hope will compel you to risk. Don't take it lightly.

Pause to consider whether we are right about these causes of life, and whether they are strong enough for you to risk setting aside your fears.

—m—

The vehement diagnosis came in a single word: Cancer. Suddenly, like a flock of startled birds, thoughts of both life and impending death took flight. Over the coming weeks with elemental and raw power life, and all that causes life, becomes the priority. Our task was to find ways to set aside fear.

> Twice a month, in the early afternoon, before strength fades, a group of people living with cancer met in Big Timber, Montana. One day, Patty, who became adept at helping other uninsured members find ways to not despair, spoke of the day she saw her horse run, promised with tears in her eyes that she was going to live to see it run again. A teacher was heading to England to see a Shakespeare play. Another began to save for a trip to Latin America that could only happen if her chemotherapy turned the tide. Our gatherings were an advanced course in life best understood by those from whom life was almost snatched away. There was no room for pretending, no opportunity for denial; but in the midst of the stories, between the moments of laughter and the silences, when we reached for a box of tissues to wipe away our tears, there was plenty of room for life.
>
> One day a member, Judy, gave the group a stunning quilt she had handsewn and eloquently named, "Migrating to the Light." The red squares signified anger at the diagnosis; the black signified despair; the blue stood for serenity; the green jealousy at those who do not have such an affliction; the yellow and white squares at the top signified life. "This is for you," she said to us, and we fought back our tears. She had spoken about life.
>
> Truly, life is not a new idea. We have many teachers.
>
> *Larry*

I've been deeply affected by seminal thinkers who have written about life: Jonas Salk,[1] Aaron Antonovsky,[2] John Wesley,[3] and Walter Rauschenbusch.[4] They poured their few years into the stream of life leaving it stronger and richer, just as each of us will do. It seems that every generation needs some help in remembering the point of it all: that life that passes through us and beyond us.

I'm especially indebted to Jonas Salk's radical curiosity about life, and his playful hope for an "epidemic of health." Salk respected the swarming intelligence of viral epidemics that find ways to move around the planet adapting all the time to find the niches here and there amid the weakness of human society.[5] Opportunistic, unpredictable, persistent, and from time to time deadly to their human hosts, viruses would seem to have all the high cards. But humans actually carry on quite a respectable fight—not because we can be like viruses, but because we have another set of life strategies. For instance, while we don't reproduce very often, we do so in the context of complex bonds of nurture, dependency, and affection that persist "in sickness and in health." We humans don't swarm, but we do recognize patterns, analyze, reflect, remember, plan, and sometimes act rationally. We also act with passion and hope undergirded by our powerful ability to create symbols and ritual that hold us up and pull us forward. And, of course, we're really, really good with all sorts of tools. Over the last several hundred thousand years, the epidemic of human health has competed quite well with viral life. While we should give due respect to avian flu and AIDS, the human life strategy is worth understanding. In a time when fear seems to fill up our imagination leaving no room for anything else, it is important for those that love at all to think that life may pass through us and beyond us. Maybe we can be part of a renewed epidemic of health.

This book should be enough to open you up to the possibility of life. You'll probably want to test what you see against your full bookshelf before you leap in and go changing your life. But maybe not. Maybe you'll see what you've been sensing all along, and find confirmation of what you already know. If so, you'll notice that you're not alone. There are people working on life in the most re-markable ways, every bit as clever as the urban raccoons I've come to admire in downtown Memphis. People are working on life in hos-pitals and in neighborhoods from northern Zambia to South Chicago. It turns out that life is relevant to AIDS, suicide, and the re-vitalization of urban communities. It is a useful way for clergy to rediscover how to lead a life of pastoral excellence, just as it helps young nurses enter into the first years of a life of healing. You'll find just enough about these webs of transformation that you can recog-nize the ones around you and those that may have already been part of you. This will probably feel more like remembering than discov-ering. If so, we'll be grateful that we've been a part of your life for a few hours. Let's go for a walk around the neighborhood.

A Note on Reading This Book

We are grateful to have two minds at work in this book and hope you will benefit from and enjoy joint perspectives on the Leading Causes of Life. You'll find both Gary and Larry's experiences, ideas, and writings on the Leading Causes of Life—and for the most part it doesn't make any difference which is which. Most of the book is a combination of their two voices and will be presented as first-person plural (we). For clarity, Larry's writings are printed in gray boxes.

CHAPTER ONE
Choose Life

I want to talk about life, not death. I now see that I've been trying to make that simple statement for at least 15 years.

In 1992 I was working at The Carter Center's Africa Program helping with new elections. A few months after being there, I was asked to start a new program at The Carter Center linking the powerful sciences of public health to the strengths of faith communities. The simple idea was that the 100 million or so people who show up in worship every month should have some impact on preventing premature death.[6] Two-thirds of deaths before age 65 turn out to be preventable by fairly mundane social policies and pro-health personal decisions.[7] It seemed obvious that religious folks were in positions to influence these policies and decisions at personal, family, neighborhood, and even national levels. Unknown to me, a grant had been written under which The Carter Center received $1.5 million dollars to create not a think tank, but a *do* tank that would go after congregations and hold them accountable to do all that they could do.[8] President Carter called the program the Interfaith Health Program (IHP), and we immediately started having conversations with communities across the U.S. This eventually led across the globe to Europe and Africa, as well as to public health institutions like the Centers for Disease Control and Prevention at home in Atlanta.

It all made great sense to me. But I didn't know if the logic that made such sense to public health people would make any sense to those in the pews. I asked Lanny Peters, our preacher at Oakhurst Baptist Church, whether I could borrow the pulpit for a Sunday and try to preach a sermon on public health. Oakhurst is the kind of place where really odd questions tend to be treated respectfully, so he said yes. In many ways, this book is a long footnote to one of the things I said accidentally in that first sermon as: "We must make the choices that lead toward life." The words of Deuteronomy urging humanity to choose life, which had been gestating in my heart for so long, surfaced with startling urgency, even though I had no idea what I was asking and certainly no idea how much I didn't know. (See Deuteronomy 30:19b.)

> # Choosing life is a lot murkier than fighting death. A stopped war is not the same as peace. Life is different than non-death.

I thought of that odd passage in Luke 19 about Jesus weeping because Jerusalem did not know what led to peace, I now know that we have little idea about what leads to life. And Jesus still weeps.

We must make the choices that lead toward life.

But how do you choose life when all we really have are tools to fight death? How do we even talk about it?

Choosing life is a lot murkier than fighting death in exactly the same way that trying to wage peace is a lot murkier that trying to stop a war. A stopped war is not the same as peace. Life is different than non-death.

Twenty-first-century medicine has an extraordinary array of tools, techniques, and technologies that are effective in fighting death and disability. Many in my congregation, including my wife Karen, routinely save three or four lives a week using the astonishing gifts of modern medicine. Some of us have had our own lives saved a few times. We are filled with nothing but gratefulness for those gifts. We also know a lot about preventing all sorts of terrible bodily things, some of which we don't notice nearly as much, but should be even more grateful about. We even know how to eliminate some diseases like polio and smallpox. The combination of public health and modern medicine has resulted in the average U.S. life expectancy in 2005

Connection brings about life; the lack of connection brings about loneliness.

being roughly 37 years longer than it was when my mother was born in 1908.[9] Thirty-seven years times billions of people is a very big deal indeed. This trend has not happened everywhere in the world, of course. AIDS is reversing this dramatically in Africa. But the exception proves the possibility.

In rural ministry the word 'neighbor' is best understood as a verb. It was not surprising that after the fires burned over 200,000 acres in August and September, 2006, the Montana churches of Big Timber put together a talent show to raise money for the ranchers who had lost their pastures, their fences, their very livelihood. At the talent show an eighth-grade girl sang, a fiddler played, several choirs took to the stage, a pianist shared his music, and before the evening was over they had raised nearly $10,000—and once again turned the word 'neighbor' into a powerful verb. Rural ministry, indeed all ministry, is about connection. Life without connection would be strange indeed. "You have to be part of the life of the town to live here," a friend said to me after musing that some who relocate for the beauty of the mountains, find life in a small town to be anything but easy if they fail to establish the connections necessary for neighboring. Connection brings about life; the lack of connection brings about loneliness. On Sunday mornings we gather to see how the life of our church connects with the wider world, and how we as individuals can best neighbor each other. It is all about the life-giving relationships.

Wonderful as it is, connection alone is not enough. Just after the service begins, connection quickly leads to coherence as we dare to say, "God is not the author of chaos." We risk saying that stories first told 3,000 years ago provide enough coherence to center our lives. We do not do this naïvely, or assuming that coherence is strong enough to deny death. We know all too well that the tragedies of life cannot be avoided just because we share a world of meaning that seeks to be mindful of God and neighbor. We do not know why Abby, a 13-year-old girl in our town, could not survive the infection that swept her life away. But we do know that the more than 300 e-mails sent to Abby, her sister, and parents were all searching for coherence in a time of deep sadness as an entire town hoped against hope and then gathered to mourn her death. We know that following and trusting the thread of coherence as individuals and as a community leads us into life and past the thickets of circumstance that so easily entrap us.

On Sunday mornings and in our ministries throughout the week we go out of our way to renew hope. "Fear not," we hear over and over again from biblical texts in which there is plenty to fear. "Fear not," we hear suddenly believing that the words were written just for us. When all seems hopeless, we know we must begin migrating towards hope or we will be overtaken by despair. Recently, St. Vincent's Hospital in Billings, Montana, asked me to lead a weekly service in the chapel that would be called "Time for Hope." A woman who had been diagnosed with cancer saw a poster announcing the service at the hospital coffee shop and decided to attend.

"I saw the sign and decided I could use some hope," she said. So did the mother who had been waiting for her infant child to be taken out of Intensive Care. So did the woman whose husband was about to be released. Would she have the necessary strength to care for him?

Not long ago my wife, Connie, asked our oldest son how he kept hope alive when the earth as we know it seems to be vanishing before our very eyes, when war follows war, and his disability continues its relentless march. "What's the option?" he said. "Holding on to hope is all we can do." It is hope that inspires good news, that looks past circumstance, and that insists on a new creation.

Larry

Creation brings us to agency. Death is stationary, but life is not. One thing leads to the next. In the film *Jurassic Park*, the cloned dinosaurs were bred to be sterile. But to the astonishment of the scientists, they were reproducing anyway. "Life finds a way," said the mathematician with a smile.[10] Life does indeed find a way. A congregation may either dwindle or may suddenly burst in growth; either way change is at work as life finds a way. It would be impossible to tell the stories of our lives without paying attention to the way one event sets the stage for the next, how one decision inspires the next, and how these transitions move our lives along. Sometimes we are the agents of change; sometimes life itself sweeps through our lives with the power of a hurricane, the diagnosis of cancer, or the loss of a job. Sometimes this concept of agency takes on serious tones,

Blessing provides the leverage that changes the way we view the world. It is something we can receive, it is something we can give away.

and sometimes it is as pure and powerful as play. Agency, for example, describes the way a breeze moves the arms of a mobile and the act of the artist that created the mobile, as well as the constellations that inspired the mobile crossing overhead each night.

There has never been a sermon that wasn't intended to inspire agency. Clergy learn to gently smile when a parishioner says, "Nice sermon." They would so much rather hear, "I am going to forgive my neighbor" or "I am going to rearrange my priorities" or "I am going to see what I can do."

Needless to say, blessing is also a necessary part of life's language so eloquently rehearsed each week in worship services throughout the earth. How many times have we as clergy been asked to bless, and how many times in our callings have we asked someone, "Could you use a blessing?" No service ends without the *bene dicte*, the "good word," intended to send us into a "torn and troubled world" full of renewed hope, renewed meaning, renewed connections, and renewed courage. Blessing provides the leverage that changes the way we view the world. It is something we can receive, it is something we can give away, but we cannot bless ourselves.

Think about life and the story you find will inevitably nest in these five Leading Causes of Life: connection, coherence, agency, blessing, and hope. When you tell the story we believe you will be speaking the language of life.

We have seen how communities are energized when they find a sense of shared purpose known as coherence; when hope fuels the change known as healing; when blessings provide unimaginable opportunity; when way does indeed lead to way just as the poet Robert Frost said it would. We believe that you will find the Leading Causes of Life are constantly at work behind the scenes. The neighborhood may appear discouraged, but talk to its inhabitants and it doesn't take long to discover a depth of connection between neighbors and the presence of hope. When it seems like nothing is happening, it turns out that life is speaking, asking us to pay attention to its rhythms, its presence in our lives.

We believe you can discern and confirm this in your own life.

Could not the story of your life be told by asking: What connections have inspired you and shaped you along the way? Who neighbored you? Who were your teachers?

If you could trace the thread of coherence in your life, what world of meanings would you find? Sometimes the thread is easy to follow and detect; sometimes it is full of twists and turns and paradoxes that are all part of the search for meaning.

What have you done, and what has been done to you?

Where has hope come to your rescue?

Where in your life have you been blessed, and how have you blessed others?

Your story would take a long time to tell. So would the stories of the institutions that have shaped your life because they have also been touched by the five Leading Causes.

Along the way your story would be told both by what is and by what is not. You will think of the connections that vanished just when you thought they were the most reliable. You will review the actions that turned out to have nothing to do with life, even though at the time they seemed to be full of promise. Simply in the telling of your story you will recognize how integral the Leading Causes have been.

—ᴍ—

Study death no more. What do you think about when you speak life and study death no more?

That's the question that has set me on a journey toward life. I've wondered if there is any way to think about life with the precision and rigor that we use when we try to postpone death. Are there causes of life to organize our thoughts and guide our actions?

In science we learn something causes an action. In my case, a speech caused me to turn toward life and away from death.

Two years ago I shared the platform at an academic meeting on disparities held in Milwaukee. David Williams, a preeminent University of Michigan sociologist, named the evil of racial disparities so completely that death filled the space in all its malevolent power. Faced with the glacial weight of racism across the generations, what could I say next? It was so clear to me that if death defines our efforts, it wins every damn time. Why are we even surprised? As you know, a lot of people aren't surprised. They don't expect to win, and thus don't even show up to fight the big ones: race, class, greed, and environmental erosion. Why would they if death is going to get the last word?

> I've wondered if there is any way to think about life with the precision and rigor that we use when we try to postpone death. Are there causes of life to organize our thoughts and guide our actions?

I junked my planned speech and decided that I wasn't going to talk about death any more. I moved to the podium humming a recycled Baptist spiritual, "I'm gonna study death no more, I'm gonna study death no more. I'm gonna lay my body down, and study death no more." Being the true son of my atonal father, I couldn't actually sing; but at least I could speak without notes, and did.

For the first time, that day I spoke about being accountable to life, and I noticed ten minutes into the speech, that people's posture changed. Academicians are not normally given to attentiveness; but this group was riveted, sitting up, leaning in, and listening. I've seen the same hopeful change every time I've had the chance to talk about life. I can assure you it isn't that I'm such a great speaker, but that the subject of life reminds people of what is most powerful. They remember the point of their lives, and it makes all the difference.

Our imagination is so filled with resisting death that we hardly know what else to think about. Fear crowds everything else, leaving no room in our imagination, no logic other than simple resistance, and no virtue other than tenacity. If President Franklin Roosevelt was right and the only thing we have to fear is fear itself, then how can we turn from fear and death to life? Like the speech that caused me to speak of life and use its language, I asked myself: Are there causes of life that can be known just as concretely?

> Our imagination is so filled with resisting death that we hardly know what else to think about.

In health science it is a very big claim to say that something is a cause. It says, "This is what is really going on here. No matter what you wish or hope for, this is what causes that." It is in some ways a religious claim.

I'll skip the footnotes and save the intellectual scaffolding for later. I want to tell you that once our imagination turns away from studying death we begin to notice that death isn't the only thing going on at all. Life is going on, too.

> Once our imagination turns away from studying death we begin to notice that death isn't the only thing going on at all. Life is going on, too. It's not just us against death. It's life against death. And that turns out to be a fair fight.

It's not just us against death. It's life against death. And that turns out to be a fair fight. You aren't delusional to want a piece of that fight.

Every time I've spoken on this idea, someone comes up afterward and tells me about some body of research and practice that is about life. Almost always the group is working on the margins of its field, exploring and asking what could be, what should be, if life is to be

A Difference in Perspective: Life's View

Death Sees	Life Sees	So What?
Cancer And its losses that feed fear and separation.	Experience of Connection. Focus on essential meaning, choices and actions to be made, hope for the things that last	Life language focuses on what is left, not what is lost. "Patient" remains a human who is still a blessing. Life focuses on the rest of the body that doesn't have cancer and asks what it can do.
Homicide And the fear of violence, revenge, desire for separation.	Life laments loss, but focuses on those still alive. Life sees connections, the possibility of forgiveness and repentance. Life sees those who love.	Life focuses on breaking the cycle of incoherent revenge. It looks at the connections among all involved and sees possibilities of a web of blessing. It seeks the health of all involved through practical choices and actions that give hope.
AIDS Deaths And millions of hopeless children.	Millions of connections that find coherence through the choices and actions that give kids a chance.	The expectation of life focuses programs beyond animal level survival needs toward education and support for new kinds of social connections that allow life to thrive.
Aging And all the fears of dependency and frailty and isolation.	A whole generation living long enough to be the elders we need. It notices that most elders have high capacity until the very end of their much-longer lives.	Life expects elders to be a blessing for the community, filled with agency not just a dependency. Life programs around the agency of elders and gives them choices that harness their capacities. Life builds new webs of connections from the existing ones.

both fully engaged and treasured. This idea is working on the margins of adolescent risks, suicide, oncology, churches, community development, and business management. You name it and there are all these positive paradigms churning away. You have to look, but they are there.

What I've found is that life is strong, vital, irrepressible, adaptive, and lively. It is enough to make you burst into laughter, delight, celebration, and dance. Hear the Easter joke: "Why do you search for the living among the dead?" And don't miss the punch line: "He's alive!"

—⚉—

If you want to learn something, teach it. For more than a year the Leading Causes of Life had been emerging as an idea through discussions, presentations, and even academic lectures. But no audience had been simultaneously confronted by it and the language of death until a Tuesday night in May, 2006, at the North 40 Cafe in Big Timber, Montana when Larry read a draft introduction to this book. He relates that evening's experience as follows:

> People had heard the book would be called the *Leading Causes of Life* and were intrigued by the title. I had been living away from Big Timber for over a year while undergoing rehabilitation for my strokes, so the assembled crowd wanted to both learn about the book and catch up with me on what I'd been doing with the life I'd so nearly lost.
>
> The opening line in my draft was, "Life has a language." The North 40 crowd was both a comfort and a challenge to me. I felt comforted because a community of neighbors surrounded me. The fact that they were well-versed in life challenged me because the words I read had to ring true. If they could not stand the test of authenticity when measured in the hearts of the listeners I knew I would be letting us all down.
>
> As the reading went on, I sensed that in the very fabric of their lives they knew all about connection, coherence, agency, hope, and blessing. I came to a part of the Introduction

which tried to distinguish the language of life from its counterpart, the language of death that is wrapped in hopelessness, loneliness, incoherence, action that can do no more than pinpoint what is wrong and is unable to speak a creative or healing word, and an utter absence of blessing. This language of death surrounds us on all sides. Turn on the news, read the headlines in this morning's paper; and the stories are written in the language of death that rivets our attention and can't help but distract us from life.

It is odd, perhaps even tragic that the language of life that asks us to live is so easily lost in the background noise of our culture. Indeed, speaking, much less singing, the language of life in a world in which so much is awry seems foolish. In this day and age, after all, one must be a realist. In fact, truth itself has become synonymous with getting "down to the bare-boned facts," and the abstract nouns that we have deemed the Leading Causes of Life seem almost Pollyannaish. The language of death accuses hope of covering up the facts, coherence as a matter of no more than circumstance, and blessing as a nice idea but one that can't change the world. There is a language of life, but the language of death is far easier to speak.

Not long ago Gary and I received the following e-mail outlining Montana's social inequities. Each sentence is an indictment begging for a governor, a legislature, a church, a city, a county, to come to its senses:

> "Nationally, Montana ranks 45th in per capita income, 44th in population, 5th in teen death rate, 4th in size, 3rd in alcohol-related traffic fatalities, 2nd in suicides, and 1st in fatal vehicle crashes on rural roads. Every 48 hours someone in Montana commits suicide. These incidences are particularly high in rural areas where social isolation is common and access to mental health services is limited or non-existent. One in five Montana families has a family member affected with a serious mental illness. Stigma and discrimination keep many affected individuals from disclosing their illness. Research studies have shown that 90 percent of the people who commit suicide suffer from undiagnosed, untreated, or inadequately treated mental illness.

"The Montana Department of Corrections (DOC), one of the largest treatment providers for mental illness, will soon become one of the largest chemical dependency providers in the state. Currently there are more people living with mental illness housed in Montana jails and prisons than in the state mental health facilities. In a survey conducted in 2000, a total of 12 percent of Montana's 2,233 inmates housed in facilities responding to the survey were in counseling, and 21.4 percent were receiving psychotropic medications."[11]

This previous study was an autopsy really, with not a single a word of life in the entire piece. Despair reigned supreme. As I read the report aloud I could feel a pall descend upon the group at the North 40. It was as though life itself had been sucked right out of us. We knew the report was undeniably true and that it demanded the attention of the governor, the legislature, the churches and communities of our state; but they were the words of a medical examiner. The North 40 crowd seemed to say, "That's not the language of life!" They were not looking to deny the brokenness so accurately portrayed in the study, and they were not trying to pretend that everything was fine when it so clearly wasn't. But we sensed that the healings required to reverse tragic statistics will have to be framed in the language of life. If we only repeat a litany of despair, no matter how accurate they may be, we will never heal the injustices that beset us or heal the illnesses that afflict us. After all, Jesus did not say to Lazarus, "This is why you died." He said, "Lazarus, come out" (John 11:43, NRSV).

A seminary professor came forward after the reading to share an experience.

"I led a class last year about the state of women in the world," she said. "The more we read the more depressing it became. The readings were overwhelming. At the end of the class I scheduled some time for us to recover from the truths we had encountered. I knew we needed to take time to summon strength and gather ourselves. If we hadn't done that we would have all been left in a state of despair. Now I know what we were doing. We needed to claim the language of life."

The professor's search reflected her students' search for connection, coherence, agency, blessing, and hope powerful enough to transcend and change circumstance. All they needed were the gifts of time, place, and community in which life could be recovered.

I had sent the Montana autopsy and introductory chapter to the Rev. Ted Erickson, a man who dedicated his career to the prophetic ministries of the United Church of Christ. Ted's response to the material was much the same as that of the seminary professor.

"When you mentioned the title of your book several months ago, I thought it was great, but what would it mean?" he said. "Now I know. Every day I receive emails from concerned critics outlining all that is wrong with this administration or this society. In the main, I agree with them, but I also experience a deadening sense of dissociation. You have given my experience a language—it is the language of death. We need a language of life."

Larry

—⁊⁊⁊—

If you focus on life and bring its discussion into the center, you'll find five vital Leading Causes of Life always show up like faithful friends. If you took all the marginalized congregations—sort of like my beloved Oakhurst—you'll find the same five. If you look at the most successful efforts to do anything with kids in the toughest neighborhoods, jails, or jungles, you'll recognize the same five again: connection, coherence, agency, blessing, and hope.

Death is simple compared to life. Although there are hundreds of thousands of names for it, basically in death something stops working. The breaking is simple; that which is broken—life—is highly complex. Life is complex because it has many moving parts that exist in exquisitely rich relationships with each other. We live in connections; we thrive in webs of meaning that make reality coherent; we flourish in our capacities to work together on things that matter; we bloom in our experience of giving and receiving

> We live in connections; we thrive in webs of meaning that make reality coherent; we flourish in our capacities to work together on things that matter; we bloom in our experience of giving and receiving blessings across generations; and we prosper as we are drawn toward hope.

blessings across generations; and we prosper as we are drawn toward hope. Connection, coherence, agency, blessing, and hope create space for each other, and jointly create the space in which life thrives. Life works wonderfully well.

The Leading Causes of Life offer us no plan for private (or tribal) triumph. This is just not how life works. The testimony of theology, ecology, and health science is that the only way we live, at all, is together. The Bible speaks of the vine and branches because there is no other way. It doesn't work every time in every place, but it is the only thing that works at all.

> The testimony of theology, ecology, and health science is that the only way we live, at all, is together. The Bible speaks of the vine and branches because there is no other way. It doesn't work every time in every place, but it is the only thing that works at all.

Life is no easy thing to work with, either. While people find the language of life inspiring, many find the pathway offered here frustrating, unpredictable, and complicated. The more a person is under pressure to find a quick fix, the more frustrating the Leading Causes of Life will probably be. I learn this every time I sit down with powerful people who are in their positions because they've convinced somebody that they can fix important things. This is most evident in academics. The justification of an academic degree seems to be that it equips one with tools to fix things of increasing complexity: a college degree for institutional kinds of problems; a master's degree for bigger ones; and some variety of "D" (doctor of philosophy, education, or ministry) for the really big ones. Of course, for my body I want someone with a "D" in medicine and hopefully some extra training on top of it.

If one assembles a whole gaggle of "D"-equipped people into a faculty, the pressure of their respective expectations mounts to cosmic levels, as does their capacity for self-delusion—and I speak as the member of several faculties.

I once met with the president of a seminary to talk about how health and faith are coming together in the life of the church in America. He knew that I worked in the health field these days, and he sort of forgot that I'd been in a sanctuary for more than half a century of Sundays. So he felt it necessary to explain that the crisis of the church was so profound today—the congregations so weak and distracted—that they needed programs that could "plug-and-play," like a Game Boy the kids in the back seats of cars use. I finally realized what he meant by this: that congregations need something (ideas, Scripture, sermons) that can work on their hearts and minds right away without requiring any new moral, ideological, or philosophical shifts. Who wouldn't want that?

I'm a bit on the geeky side and have drawers filled with electronic things that were supposed to plug-and-play. It would never dawn on me to think of anything less likely to happen in a normal congregation. So I thought he was kidding. I stared at him for a few beats, waiting for him to chuckle at his own joke. But he never did. Like others living their lives in a hurry, he would be slow to think the idea of Leading Causes of Life could be realistic in such desperate and furiously competitive times as ours.

While everyone wishes that transformation could be so simple, the whole "plug-and-play" metaphor is useless with anything that involves humans, especially when you try to think about congregations or communities. Computer programmers are able to write plug-and-play games because they are doing so in the context of dependable, standardized operating systems and hardware standards which assure that their little gizmos will, in fact, plug and will, in fact, play. No one knows exactly how many, but there are at least 4,000 religious denominations in the United States alone, each with its own "operating system."[12] Those numbers disguise the actual chaos since many congregations act with the autonomy of a denomination, while many denominations act with the timidity and low function of a small congregation. It may be easier to plug in a seminary president and watch him or her play because there are only a few hundred seminaries and a more predictable set of challenges to play with. Imagining that we can save the church with plug-and-play programs is a counsel of despair; perhaps one of the final gasps of a body that deserves a dignified burial.

> The most basic thing to get right in life is the question. It increases the odds a great deal if you hang around people with a history of asking great questions. And the question only leads toward life if it is in the language of life.

The most basic thing to get right in life is the question. It increases the odds a great deal if you hang around people with a history of asking great questions. And the question only leads toward life if it is in the language of life. For this to be more than happy talk, that language requires disciplined powers of observation. The Leading Causes of Life is not based on what "should be." The five causes are not platitudes. They do not represent ideals. Larry and I are not saying that life should help us connect, that it should have meaning, that it should be hopeful, that it should be a blessing, and that it should lead to action. We are saying that it actually does all five. We have noticed that life happens when these five Leading Causes are present and that their absence contributes to the void so many of us feel. We have seen that churches thrive when they connect with a mission, when their members and friends learn how to "neighbor." We have seen institutions gain new life when they spend time building relationships; we have seen healing move to a higher level when it builds trust between doctor and patient, hospital and community.

—⁊⁊⁊—

When human beings are in difficult times we hope for change, even for transformation. We soon learn that transformation is not about resisting death, but about nurturing life. We tend to tell the old, old story of life. So, transformation can't be understood using the logic tools of assessment, skill-building, and organizational development that are essentially based on death. For instance, much government policy is driven by the leading causes of death, which seems to make sense because it can be quantified. Systematically pursuing population-scale strategies for death reduction and disease prevention has been fabulously successful and compelling. But they are quite limited in their logic of dealing with what Marshall Kreuter calls "wicked problems" that seem to defy resolution.[13] They are even more unsatisfying in dealing with what I might call "vital opportunities." We need more of what's alive, not just less of what's dying. I want to study death no more. I want to understand and be drawn by the Leading Causes of Life, not the leading causes of death. But the question remains: what exactly do we think about when we're not thinking about death? How do we come up with a theory of life?

A few years ago, I spent some time with a group of Christian ethicists who were trying to come up with the next generation of ethics beyond the "Just War Theory." As most of us know, the "Just War Theory" refers to moral and political doctrines that promote the view that war can be "just" if given satisfactory criteria are met. I was not highly qualified to do that work, but participated on behalf of the Carter Center. Because of President Carter's reflected glory, I found myself expected to be one of the experts. So I forged ahead beyond my qualifications. I suggested to the group that what the world really needed was a very simple list that any bumbling politician on their way to the podium could remember— a list of the steps that had to be done in order to say that we had truly "sought peace." You might remember that when President George W. Bush was trying to explain what the heck the United States was doing invading Iraq, he felt compelled to

We need more of what's alive, not just less of what's dying. I want to study death no more. I want to understand and be drawn by the Leading Causes of Life, not the leading causes of death. But the question remains: what exactly do we think about when we're not thinking about death? How do we come up with a theory of life?

give some passing attention to the Just War Theory. I'm sure the "just peace" ethicists had in mind a higher standard, which might have slowed him down a smidgen. Or maybe if it would not have slowed him down at all, it would have speeded up the opposition. If we had been familiar with this list of peace-seeking strategies, we would have noticed the train wreck before it left the station and perhaps been compelled to seek peace more aggressively than we did. I joined hundreds of people in a protest on the courthouse square on the night of the invasion of Iraq, and we reminisced to our children about the old Vietnam protest days. When we tried to schedule another protest, we all looked at our Palm Pilots and realized it would be difficult to squeeze it in. It was clear that we had not been fully seized by the "just peace ethic" and so the war continues as I write.

> We need a life logic that is simple and compelling, more powerful than our lethargic moral inertia.

We need a life logic that is simple and compelling, more powerful than our lethargic moral inertia. We need a theory that could be scribbled on the back of a business card—even under pressure. Then, when we're in the midst of a hard meeting trying to figure out what to do with some terrible problem, we could remember the five Leading Causes of Life and be compelled to frame our work around them, not death. The ethicists came up with ten new components for a Just Peace Strategy. Ten is more than I can remember and more that fits on the back of my business card. So let's see if we can keep track of five and call them The Leading Causes of Life.

—⚏—

We are seeking the causes of life in a time marked by profound disorientation, deep confusion, and the seemingly infinite capacity to fear. A wise friend who knew I was trying to think about life, recommended an old book by Jonas Salk, *Survival of the Wisest*.[14] Salk argues that the survival of the species is now dependent on the maturing of our culture away from competition and toward the virtues needed for survival. In the time of the great turning—which is our

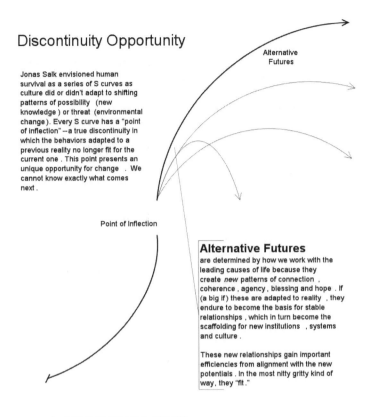

Discontinuity Opportunity

Alternative
Futures

Jonas Salk envisioned human
survival as a series of S curves as
culture did or didn't adapt to shifting
patterns of possibility (new
knowledge) or threat (environmental
change). Every S curve has a "point
of inflection" --a true discontinuity in
which the behaviors adapted to a
previous reality no longer fit for the
current one . This point presents an
unique opportunity for change . We
cannot know exactly what comes
next .

Point of Inflection

Alternative Futures
are determined by how we work with the
leading causes of life because they
create *new* patterns of connection ,
coherence , agency , blessing and hope . If
(a big if) these are adapted to reality , they
endure to become the basis for stable
relationships , which in turn become the
scaffolding for new institutions , systems
and culture .

These new relationships gain important
efficiencies from alignment with the new
potentials . In the most nitty gritty kind of
way , they "fit ."

Jonas Salk, Survival of the Wisest , (Harper and Row) 1973.

only hope—we will only survive if we are wise. This is not the same as saying that only the wise among us will survive. None of us will, if all of us don't act wisely as a whole.

Salk understands that every species faces critical points in its development when it must adapt to fundamental changes in its environment or it will no longer fit. When it can no longer be fit it will die. Just remember that he means us: we will die.[15] Salk called this time between times "the point of inflection" and in other places "the point of discontinuity" which we will cross only with wisdom. That wisdom he speaks of is not wired into our synapses; it only exists in the culture of life among us.

You can feel this "point" as you trace an "S" curve in the air with your hand. As you trace one arc and then the next, you will feel a brief space between—the point where the line inflects into a different arc. You can feel the brief space where one becomes the next, where it is not at all clear what that next curve will be. A cultural "point of discontinuity" may be a couple hundred years long, while an organizational inflection may only be a dozen years or so. But in each case, there is a definite shift from one trajectory to the next. Understanding the dynamic Leading Causes of Life is much more important in a time of inflection or discontinuity than during a stable, predictable time. Rote memory will serve in a stable time, but only the wisdom beyond mere intelligence can serve us in a time of inflection. To realize that we are in a time of discontinuity is hopeful (to me, at least). It turns on the lights so that we can see that we live in a time that is awkward, but not hostile. We can see opportunity, and the value of new appreciation and alignment. Naming the discontinuity chases away those attracted to the plug-and-play hopes that we know are too brittle for these times. Discontinuity is for grown-ups.

> To realize that we are in a time of discontinuity is hopeful. It turns on the lights so that we can see that we live in a time that is awkward, but not hostile.

Grown-ups notice that the old fashioned tools of violence are of little help in navigating a time of discontinuity. Violence and force can destroy a point of inflection but can't find a trajectory across one. Archbishop Desmond Tutu, veteran of apartheid's cold hand and the radical discontinuity that replaced it, was stating the obvious when he said, "Anything war can do, peace can do better."[16] In a time of inflection, old social and institutional systems disintegrate, even when they fight with all the old tools that worked so well for them in the earlier era. Those institutions that survive change will discover new potential driven by patterns of hope, and a confidence more appropriate to the emerging era. Boundary zones are broken open even more as old institutions become more loosely connected and new ones pop up in the cracks. At first the new ones appear so weak, but sometimes the slender shoots find themselves well adapted to the new world and survive.

Jim Cochrane, my friend in Cape Town, tells of being a youth worker at a small Methodist Church during the resistance to apartheid. The pastor of that church formed a laughably fragile network called the Christian Institute that stood against the fearsome violence of apartheid with the weakness of transparency, trust, song, and truth-telling. Its leading members were banned, prohibited from even meeting with each other. Some left the country, others were killed; but the weakness of the Institute has long outlasted the brittle strength of the apartheid government. Indeed, the Institute took to heart the counterintuitive Christian message that in weakness one becomes strong.

In a time of discontinuity any one part of a system is aware of its own change, but often unaware that the change is generalized between systems. We are so aware of the discontinuity within the church that we hardly notice that nearly all major institutions are inflecting, too. Some people call it tunnel vision. In health care we are so aware of our changing world that we fail to notice that every other part of the community is changing, too. We think our discontinuity is particular and distinct, when it only reflects a more general time in between times.

The next inflection—the alternative future—is determined by a critical mass of what we call boundary leaders. They often do their work as the Christian Institute did. They don't focus on the old pattern, but focus on the new. These leaders create new patterns of fear, hope, and confidence. If—a big if—these hopes, fears, and confidences are adapted to the actual Leading Causes of Life, then they endure and become the basis for stable relationships. Those relationships in turn become the scaffolding for new institutions, systems, and cultures on the other side of discontinuity. Who knows how long that bridge over discontinuity must be? We don't and can't know on this side of it. But given the radical nature of our current discontinuities—I'm thinking of global warming and global culture conflict—we had better settle down for a long time in transit. Think of the amino acids that survive a comet's journey, and trust that life will find a way.

The relationships formed along the way help us find important efficiencies from their alignment with these new potentials. In practical ways, as our old disciplines break apart, we find new insights that are only possible by blending our insights. And the relationships make possible innovations reflecting multiple intelligences needed to perceive the path toward hope and survival. Out of the terrible brokenness of Dr. Martin Luther King Jr.'s death in Memphis, religious leaders formed the Metropolitan Inter-Faith Association (MIFA), which has found amazing power and innovation at exactly the place where others found only despair. In the most nitty-gritty kind of way, the life-seeking relationships born in the time of discontinuity are "fit" to live. And so they do.

—◊◊◊—

In a time of discontinuity it is important to recognize the pains of birth from the pains of death—no mean feat. It helps to have a theory about what is going on so you can recognize patterns among what would otherwise look like total disconnection and chaos. Sometimes, early in the process of turning from one era to the next, it is too much to expect clear vision. Maybe we can only hope for imagination which, tested against time, may mature into a vision we will need. That sounds like a very modest goal, but it may be enough to gather around. Even imagination needs a seed of a theory so we can distinguish it from pure fantasy untethered from the ground on which we walk.

> It isn't just you against death, but life against death. The Leading Causes of Life are tough, smart, and built for complexity and chaos. These causes are up against the causes of death, which are, by comparison, simple, predictable, and mean. Now this is a fair fight.

Discontinuity holds open the possibility of both death and transformation. But it views stability as unnatural and impossible. Life seeks—and has always found—transformation. At least it has done so for the last few billion years. Transformation is different from survival for it assumes that the only way to continue is to change so that we can be fit to live. We have changed many times to get to this place. We are a very, very long way from the beginning, and thus it is likely that we are not at the end.

In linking the Leading Causes of Life to Salk's point of inflection I am pointing us toward the role of imagination, the imagination that makes possible the life of a people. The work of our prophets— Dr. King, Gandhi, Mohammed—gives a people life amid their time of discontinuity. Prophetic pathos, sorrow, and anger are driven by a sense that the people are violating their own spring of life. But far more important than naming what is broken are the prophets' cries for what has been forgotten—the source of life.

Given eyes for life, you can expect and plan for how you might align yourself and other external assets and energies with these life processes. You can act with confidence that your actions align with fundamental life principles built into the very structure of all living systems. It isn't just you against death, but life against death. The Leading Causes of Life are tough, smart, and built for complexity and chaos. These causes are up against the causes of death, which are, by comparison, simple, predictable, and mean. Now this is a fair fight.

Life connects, gives meaning, empowers, blesses, and hopes. If you are alive, something in you knows all that.

It no longer seems pathetic to want to be in that fight on the side of life. We feel deeply that in doing so we are participating in the cause of our own life. Surely, if our ancestors could hold on in far more dire circumstances, we can hold on in ours. Life connects, gives meaning, empowers, blesses, and hopes. If you are alive, something in you knows all that.

CHAPTER TWO
What's a Cause?

When I worked for Jimmy Carter, it quickly became clear that when most people would grab for a calendar to plan something, the former president would look at his watch and impatiently ask, "Why can't we have that ready by, say, four o'clock?" Although Carter had written more books than any other president, he had little appetite for theoretical discussions. He was always suspicious when we showed signs of having spent too much time just thinking about things. However, in order to know what to practice, you have to get an idea of what's going on, you need the logic that drives all the activity. Theory doesn't just help you think, it helps you see what to do.

In the Headway dayroom at St. Vincent's Hospital in Billings, Montana, I wrote five words—coherence, connection, agency, blessing, and hope—on a marker board for a group of fellow brain-injured folks and their families. The group included a 15-year-old who had been hit by a line drive baseball and spent a month or so in a coma, a 19-year-old with 90 mph tattoos who was recovering from a motorcycle accident, a woman whose brain leaked, a man whose stroke had made it impossible for him to work, and a woman learning to navigate life again after a cataclysmic accident and years of rehabilitation. We were quite a group.

"Which of these words gives you life?" I asked. "Which one jumps out at you? Which ones cause life?"

"It's connection," said one of the women, gently putting her hand on the hand of her husband. "I'm with him. It's us." We took in the steady affection that made no attempt to hide itself.

"It's hope," said the parents of the 15-year-old whose whole town had surrounded them with love and fundraisers. "It's hope because hope doesn't undo things, it just allows us to get through them."

"It's hope," echoed the motorcyclist who was just beginning to walk without his cane. "I can see it. I can feel it. It's hope."

Our discussion moved to blessing, how we couldn't control it, and didn't want to, how it didn't matter if it came from God or from another person. Either way blessing moved us to a different place.

Earlier that day, I had stopped by the flower shop in Big Timber and picked up roses from the florist. It was her usual Friday flower donation. She had survived a stroke 30 years ago and had found little support as she recreated her life. When she heard about our group she wanted to bless it by giving flowers. On that day she gave eight white roses—the color of hope. At the end of each support group, we looked around the circle and gently wondered who should receive the flowers. The group invariably "knew" where they should go and who should receive them. On that day we gave them to the family whose son had been hit by the line drive. "Here," we said, "These are for you."

> And then the psychiatric nurse-in-training noted some-
> thing important about the Leading Causes of Life. "None of
> the five involve learning a whole new way to approach life—
> they are all already at work," she said. "This should be
> taught in medical school."
>
> "Don't worry about it," I said with a smile. "That's com-
> ing."
>
> *Larry*

—⁓—

Our imaginations are so dominated by death that both our seeing and thinking are challenged. We don't expect to see life, and
then, when we do, we don't have any practice in thinking about it.
So we need a theory, or we'll be purely reactive; or even worse, stu-
pidly proactive, just blundering around.

I moved to Memphis to work as a senior executive at one of the
largest health care systems in the
United States, Methodist Le
Bonheur Healthcare. This was
totally unlike any job or situation I had ever experienced. I
had always worked in church
basements or in very small
groups of colleagues, maybe five

When you are in a radically new environment, theory helps you know what to do.

or ten people. Our health system has 10,000 staff members, not counting the 2,500 physicians who take care of our patients. I was able to
function because I have a pretty clear theory about faith, health, congregations, and community. When you are in a radically new environment, theory helps you know what to do. Most of that was laid
out in my two other books that preceded this one, *Deeply Woven Roots*
(Fortress Press, 1997) and *Boundary Leaders* (Fortress Press, 2004).
Leading Causes of Life are just such theories about life on the ground.
The ideas focus on a particular kind of life: sustained human life, the
kind that Jonas Salk was trying to be hopeful about. This is a theory
for grown-ups trying to sustain the life among those they love.

The test of a good theory is not the pleasure it brings to the mind,
but the pleasure that comes from the good work it makes possible.

Like choosing the right tool, the theory must fit the task: a hammer for nails, a saw for cutting boards, a level for getting things plumb. Our task is straightforward, and the test is whether this theory helps us live a well-lived life.

The first task of a theory is to help us understand what is going on. It is helpful to notice that one thing is associated with another like bad smells are to disease. But to actually say that the smell caused the disease is a very big step. This ill-informed idea, called "miasma theory," was held for centuries until germ theory fought its way through and finally allowed the extraordinary gifts of infectious disease prevention.[17] Until the theory changed, practice couldn't. For instance, a flawed causal theory prevented doctors dealing with childbirth fever, once the leading cause of death among women, from seeing the fact that failure to wash their hands after performing autopsies was spreading infection to their patients.[18] You would think this pattern would be noticeable but until a Viennese physician, Ignaz Philipp Semmelweis, noticed it, it was invisible. In the early 1800's, up to 30 percent of women died in childbirth. When Semmelweis instructed his student physicians to wash their hands with lime between examinations, the death rate dropped to one percent. You'd think you could get doctors to wash their hands once it was proven that their own hands were the vectors across which disease spread, but that took decades longer. (Nurses figured it out and changed their standard of washing many years before doctors.) Correct causal theory is literally the difference between life and death. There is a lesson within the lesson here and that is the

The test of a good theory is not the pleasure it brings to the mind, but the pleasure that comes from the good work it makes possible. Like choosing the right tool, the theory must fit the task: a hammer for nails, a saw for cutting boards, a level for getting things plumb. Our task is straightforward, and the test is whether this theory helps us live a well-lived life. The first task of a theory is to help us understand what is going on.

difficulty of the step between theory and widely adopted practice. The reason that there was such a lag between proof of childbirth fever theory and acceptance of the theory was the terrible job of communicating the theory by Semmelweis. He was so annoying and abrasive that his physician colleagues found him almost impossible to listen to. One could argue that bad communication is as deadly as bad theory.

The idea of leading causes is already resting on the margins of many fields of knowledge. We need to remember what is already known about life and bring it to the center. *And the first thing to remember is that life creates; death destroys.*

The idea of leading causes is already resting on the margins of many fields of knowledge. We need to remember what is already known about life and bring it to the center. *And the first thing to remember is that life creates; death destroys.*

—⁂—

There are hundreds of thousand of names for diseases and pathologies, and each of them has a diagnosis and a resulting plan of attack lodged in the logic of death, a logic of anti-death. Like the case of childbirth fever, the rigorous pursuit of the causes of death has led to many profound changes in policy and organization of human activities. This is very good. Recognizing and anticipating the causes of death has been a huge success responsible for most of the 37 added years of life we have achieved in the United States.[19] Clearly there has been great power in identifying and prioritizing the causes of death. Policy, attention, and, dare I say, imagination is attracted to thwarting the leading causes of death. Billions of dollars move as institutions and careers are built in order to approach and vanquish them.

But there is a limit to what can be perceived, understood, and acted on by focusing on the pathological phenomena of death. We just might be reaching that limit. These days the ten leading causes of death in the U.S. are: heart disease, cancer, stroke, chronic lower respiratory disease, accidents, diabetes, pneumonia/flu, Alzheimer's disease, kidney disease, and sepsis (a whole-body response to infection).[20] Each of these has battalions of professional, highly trained experts working every day to chip away at the problems. My suspicion is that the future of many of these medical and research fields would be better served by exploring a path other than the dominant death logic, the death discourse. It turns out that the vast majority of human years saved are due to fairly simple population-wide actions: mainly clean water, sanitation, good food, and shelter. These are better understood as life processes, not anti-death processes. They reflect things that contribute to life of the whole community. The right tool is one designed to look for life; the right logic is one based on causes of life. This is a matter of life and death here, so we'd better not settle for just being inspirational.

—⚒—

To say "this causes that" certainly sounds scientific, but it can also be considered close to a religious claim. The vocabulary of faith weaves humility into its most profound observations of causality. Even the most vaunted Old Testament Psalms put certainty into the future tense. The book Christians dare to call "Revelation" uses only unfettered metaphor for its most basic claims of deliverance. Jesus, who knew about life, liked parables for the heavy lifting.

Science has a rich language that permits it to go near, but rarely onto, the sacred ground of causality. In the circles of public health, we gather gigabytes of data into a revered mound on which we ascend to acclaim "association" and "correlation," but only rarely "causation." We name the associations that phenomenon keep: low birth weight is associated with all sorts of bad things later in life. A mother that smokes correlates to a child's ill health, but in ways we can't quite map with precision. We know these are related, but we hesitate to say exactly how the connection plays out. So, while we know enough to warn moms against smoking, we pause even here when saying this cigarette causes that pathology. The criminal tobacco enterprises that market these death weeds delight in this hesitation, as do their lawyers and the politicians they rent to serve their purposes. Politicians are always surprised by scientists' hesitation to claim what seems obvious, and they thrive on the humility. Like cigarettes and their effects, it is hard to miss the association between general disaster and the vastly indulgent lifestyle: the stripped coal fields, the missing glaciers, and the Argentine grapes in the grocery stores in midwinter (not to mention this coal-fired keyboard!). What exactly is the chain of causes that tie it all together? We know what is associated. But caused?

Cause matters. It aims our choices, refines our fears, and justifies our hopes. It tells us what to do. So, it's wise to go slowly when we start linking things together. This is the danger of having just a little bit of knowledge, just a smidgen of theology, just a few books on nation-building in Iraq, or just a few opinions on neighborhood-building in Memphis.

You may already be resonating to my most basic claim: that in order to know what to do, you have to think about what is giving us life as well as what is killing us. This double-mindedness is more demanding than it might seem at first, precisely because we are used to thinking mostly about problems and dying. We think grown-ups should think about bad things so that we can stop them. That's just not enough.

The problem with problems is that they are too easy compared to the vital phenomenon that has the problems. The melting of glaciers is way easier to

> **Cause matters. It aims our choices, refines our fears, and justifies our hopes. It tells us what to do.**

understand than their formation and growth. It might seem to be the same thing, but it isn't. To know how to appreciate a glacier, much less to know how to behave around one, it is important to think of how it comes to be, as well as how it disappears. If we broaden our scope even more, how important could it be to understand the life of the human communities that live around a glacier?

I have a fair bit of Norwegian blood in my veins, and a few years ago went with my family to Josetad Glacier in coastal Norway. We walked for a mile through a rounded valley past boulders larger than my Georgia cabin. Beside the trail, ran a river so cold it was hard to touch. We walked through the trees, suddenly rounded a corner into an open meadow, and stopped, staring in awe at a dirty blue wall of ice snaking up and out of sight into the mountain above us. My daughters and I scampered up impossible hills of loose rock that had clearly been broken out of the granite walls by the coming and going of the ice. Every now and then, a chunk of ice big enough to crush a bus broke off into the stream of melted water, so there were signs in three languages warning foolish humans to beware that the life of the glacier was still going on.

Ice melting wouldn't seem too hard to figure out. Any drunk at a bar grasps the concept pretty well. But appreciating the whole glacial phenomenon demands a bit more attentiveness, especially if one is curious about the people that live and used to live nearby, such as my great-great-grandfather Olie. Like many third- and fourth-borne sons in a cold time with little land, Olie Gunderson had no room to grow in his own family. The bitter winters and silly Scandinavian wars drove him across the water in a small boat to Wisconsin 150 years ago; otherwise, this book might be written in Norwegian. It would be easy to map the causes of his leaving. But how to explain the life that carried him along: the rich stew of connections and meaning, the ability to choose, and the hopes that animated such risks. In short, how to explain his life? *Or any human life?*

—⚹—

What causes the kind of life that generates life? What kind of life creates the possibility of more life? This is far more interesting than death, which simply disrupts or breaks down. Life fills up emptiness, weaves together broken pieces, and moves simplicity toward festival.

We want to look for human life not because it is entirely separate from the life of animals or glaciers, but because it is interconnected. If Jane Goodall reads this, she will certainly note that most all of our Leading Causes of Life are visible in her chimpanzees. She would probably be right, too. But our project is in service of human leaders, especially those who read books. They need to sharpen their awareness of how life happens. Humans are distinctly, if not uniquely, conscious of being conscious. This is why, technically, we are *sapiens sapiens*—knowing knowers. We want to focus that double consciousness on the causes of human social life, which generates the adaptive process of thriving. Jonas Salk wrote in *The Survival of the Wisest* that unlike the capacity of other higher order creatures, most human capacity rests in culture, not genetics or hard-wired behaviors.[21] If we are to make the choices that lead to life, we have to act wisely: to adapt our behavior in the directions that life requires. If they could speak, I am sure chimpanzees would ask humans to make the critical choices on which their lives depend, too.

To understand a life phenomenon, you have to look not for just a different list of things, but also a different kind of list. It might be fair to say it requires a more primitive imagination— the kind that, in Norway, saw gnomes and spirits under the bridges and in the high mountains. It turns out that the mountains are sort of alive and the communities of people surrounding them are certainly alive. The more we know, the more we appreciate the thriving oddness going on. The oddness of life is neither good nor bad—it's just unexpected and curious. An imagination that is tuned to life sees vital connections, upward spirals, and pregnant couplings where deduction only counts and weighs until boredom makes us blind.

What causes the kind of life that generates life? What kind of life creates the possibility of more life? This is far more interesting than death, which simply disrupts or breaks down. Life fills up emptiness, weaves together broken pieces, and moves simplicity toward festival.

We look for causes of life that:
- Generate more life and are not exhausted by it.
- Adapt and encourage ever more adaptation.
- Create ever more complex connectedness.

Our curiosity leads us to look for these causes in the spaces in between things, in the history of lives that have proceeded our own. Life causes life in this sense. This seems like circular logic, which annoys everyone except historians or biologists who largely confine themselves to living systems by definition. Curiosity leads us toward the first life and then looks beyond it into "prebiotic" processes. As intriguing as those deeper recesses of imagination may be, for the purposes of this book it is fair to state the obvious and the practical: life always springs from life.

Some scientists posit that the origins of life grew among shallow sloshing pools of amino acids. Others, thinking those pools unlikely ancestors, imagine a long cold comet ride ending with a spectacular burst of light onto what we later named Earth. Jonas Salk carried in his pocket a sliver of such a comet given to him by a dear friend. This bite-sized celestial remnant had all the necessary amino acids for human life, which reminded Salk that life will find a way.

We look for causes of life that:
- Generate more life and are not exhausted by it.
- Adapt and encourage ever more adaptation.
- Create ever more complex connectedness.

Our curiosity leads us to look for these causes in the spaces in between things, in the history of lives that have proceeded our own. Life causes life in this sense.

Personally, I find my ancestor Olie's trip from Norway hard enough. But these science folks have a way of thinking that is nothing if not hardy. The question of our earthly origins almost makes the rest of these passages seem easy by comparison. So you have to wonder why we so easily forget to look for life, when we find ourselves drifting in despair. Sometimes it's all right there in front of us—perhaps in a pool of already living stuff, or a rock from light years away. If you want to look for life, quit staring at that which will kill you.

—᠁—

Henry Turley is a man in his late sixties going on sixteen who is staring into life and its possibilities where others see squalor. Tall and nearly bald, Henry walks the streets of Uptown Memphis with a quick stride that is highly likely to deviate toward the closest human being in sight. Cop or kid, shopkeeper or cousin, Henry talks to them. I met him in a Montessori school in Harbor Town, a community of upscale homes he planted a few feet from the Mississippi River on Mud Island. That development, for which success now seems to have been inevitable, is across an inlet from a thousand acres of urban depression that he is trying to bend toward life. Unlike Harbor Town, which was a blank canvas, Uptown is cluttered with such broken pieces that an empty lot is an upgrade.

Henry and I were walking along looking for life. More specifically we were looking for life that could sustain itself after a developer's seminal "revitalization" energies are spent. This question is similar to asking about that tiny speck of life that hung on for that long, cold ride on that very specific comet that managed to hit the Earth in just the right place to splash into the perfect pond that became home to us all. That little ancestral bug was most certainly not designed for that pond, but it was close enough and adapted quickly. Sustainable life adapts. This is to say that it changes on contact over and over again. It generates, not just copies of itself, but adaptive versions of itself. It evolves, or else it dies.

In the case of what Henry wants to call Uptown, the task is harder than microbes adapting to a primal pool because humans have to think in order to adapt. The Uptown neighborhood will live only if it adapts beyond Henry's imagination toward something of its own imagination. To say that life has an imagination might be a bit too exalted for microbial particles, but it is a bare minimum for humans. No imagination means no adaptability, which means no human life. Imagination plus a few humans means you've got a shot.

We walked around the neighborhood and into a community center run by an athlete-turned-adult who was currently tending to a primal swarm of kids. A community center is a fragile place as delicate as a primal pool of microbes. I know the predictive data for these kids, and it isn't pretty. Most of these young men are more likely bound for prison than junior college. But they aren't prisoners yet. I was watching them play pretty good basketball when I noticed that the one handling the ball and driving the team was a girl. She slashed through her male opponents, passed the ball with imagination, and played defense like she meant it. She scowled a lot, but couldn't hide her delight in the game. A few minutes later, I noticed her walking out with her ball and sweatshirt, looking up and around like it was her neighborhood. I don't know anything about her except that she was alive in her own life. That's what a community like this needs: personal ownership of life and place. The sustained life of Uptown will come, if it comes at all, from the place where her imagination mingles with that of Henry to discover a way for others to find a way. I don't know what comet she rode in on, but she found a pool in which to adapt against all the odds.

The reason the community center is vital is not because it is just safe for people to gather, but because it prepares them for life outside its walls. It is a generative space, and the life it generates is viable in the real world. It doesn't just protect, although a safe space is no small thing. The center is a space that generates qualities that are capable of generating more sustained life. Schools do that sometimes, but not always. They are more likely to do so if the adults who run them are truly alive. Some of the churches are alive, too. Uptown has 70 of them, some of which date back to around the time when slaves were auctioned near the river. These churches have found a way to sustain themselves; whether they are all vital, generative spaces for the community is still a fair question. Most of the members of most of these churches, in typical Memphis fashion, do *not* live in the neighborhood with their church. People here will move away from the church's neighborhood, yet drive back to church for decades later. They may sustain the life of the congregation—pay the pastor, paint the walls—while losing all interest in, and impact on, the church's neighborhood.

> The congregations that open themselves to the real needs of people stop talking at them and start talking *with* them—coming along beside them, becoming involved in their lives.

The Carter Interfaith Health Program long ago noticed that about 10 percent of the congregations in any area do almost all of the heavy lifting in any community.[22] Heavy lifting means the difficult, complicated work of long and uncertain duration in a community.

Helping people isn't done a hundred at a time; it is done one by one by one. The congregations that open themselves to the real needs of people stop talking at them and start talking *with* them—coming along beside them, becoming involved in their lives.

The congregations end up creating the informal systems of support and change-making that end up becoming the more formal networks of social service present in almost every community in the nation. In Memphis, as I mentioned earlier, we have MIFA just down the street from our main hospital. MIFA, the Metropolitan Inter-Faith Association, was formed after Dr. King's assassination and manages a fantastic array of services from Meals on Wheels (delivering more than 2,500 hot meals to seniors at homes and congregate sites each weekday) to helping people with their power bills. In almost every community, this kind of agency is faith-related, but highly ecumenical, and usually interfaith. The congregations that participate are usually also the ones that create and sustain other kinds of specialized ministries: battered women's shelters, after-school programs, or prison release halfway houses. Pretty much the same small group of congregations finds their life in doing this kind of heavy lifting; and they are able to keep doing it year after year, decade after decade. *Deeply Woven Roots*, my earlier book on the strengths of congregations, describes the eight strengths this kind of congregation draws on to do that kind of heavy lifting.[23] I now see that those eight strengths also rest on the underlying Leading Causes of Life that are visible in the lives of the people in these heavy-lifting congregations and in the lives of the people they help.

Even though the Interfaith Health Program study usually finds that 10 percent of a community's congregations do this heavy lifting, surprisingly, that turns out to be enough. In Uptown you could wonder which seven of the seventy are really doing the kind of work from which the future might arise. I'd look right past the other 50 or 60 churches cluttering the landscape, and focus on those seven; because they are not only on life support, they are capable of supporting life. They are the generative ones. They are the quality you need to look for.

Life moves toward complex human connection and away from simplicity. The causes of life we seek enable such movement. In Memphis, sustained life depends on moving from the building of a *house*, to it becoming a *home* for a family, to the home becoming one among other homes, to those homes becoming a *neighborhood* with a shared life that generates more life. If the spiral toward complex life turns back onto itself and recoils from the diversity around it, it begins to die as its energies are wasted on its fears. A living community as a whole is the only true shepherd of this slender balance toward life. It takes a village to raise a village.

It is in our connections that life emerges and is sustained.

No *one* person managed to live anything that we'd recognize as a life, except for relatively brief and lonely passages. Even those spiritual warriors who have chosen monastic lifestyles primarily live in communities. They further prove the point by their need for rigorous training, tight discipline, and frequent failure. The rest of us humans find our lives amid the tumble of complex relationships that can be distracting and inconvenient, but are utterly vital. Either way, it is in our connections that life emerges and is sustained.

—⁂—

Life that is sustained is generative, complex, and adaptive. What causes adaptivity? The social environment in which we live creates challenges that force us to either withdraw or adapt. This makes life sound like hard slogging, but it has its pleasures. In early adolescence, boys and girls usually find each other annoying and frustratingly difficult to understand or be around. Better to stay apart except for brief, mandatory events. At some point we notice that it might be worth the trouble to entertain a

The causes of life enable and encourage complexity and move us well beyond the orbit of simplicity.

closer relationship with such complexity. About that time we notice that sexuality is anything but binary. There are six billion varieties of complexity and counting. Yikes! The complications are infinite; the choices unravel the mind, but it's worth the trouble. The social complexities challenge, release, and grip again until, quite literally, we die. The causes of life enable and encourage complexity and move us well beyond the orbit of simplicity.

Jonas Salk found hope for the species (at least a little bit) in the fact that humans are not hard wired like other forms of life.[24] Even our close associates, such as the other primates, have most of their behavior wired into their genes. This works pretty well until the environment changes: the trees get cut down, the water sours, or a band of humans comes into the neighborhood. Then these hard-wired reflexes don't work anymore. Humans have some, but not very much, of their behavior wired. Most of our roles, behaviors, and response patterns are learned, and thus capable of adapting to new learning. Salk thought we might even be capable of learning enough wisdom to adapt to profoundly new challenges such as overpopulation. The evidence is not encouraging; especially during this great species-wide self-extinction that we call global warming. But it now appears that even a little bit of economic freedom encourages families to choose to be smaller (at least once the women manage to gain any say in their own lives). Billions of choices tend toward fewer billions of people. So perhaps we'll level off at about 10 billion tightly linked friends. This is still pretty crowded, but less than we feared.

The problem is that most of those billions will still need to show some wisdom about how much junk and clutter to pump into our lives. We show pretty much no sign at all of that kind of wisdom. Not having children turns out to be an easier choice than not having a car. I have two kids and four cars. My parents raised five kids with one car. I point this out only to underline that sustained life is all about adapting to changing circumstances. Salk called this "fitness" and noted that life that is not fit for its circumstances does not continue. We can't bargain our way out of being unfit to survive. Humans have adapted to many, many circumstances along our journey, so the odds are that we'll find a way. But we probably won't drive there in separate cars.

Human life is social. There is no such thing as *one* human being. Even hermits live on a long leash tethered to a human community. From birth to death, the rest of us are almost never alone. It is life in relationships or no life at all—at least for us humans. Sea turtles can go way out to sea for years on end, wandering all over the Atlantic, but return to the same beaches they saw as hatchlings to lay eggs and start the cycle over.

Humans are less likely to wander alone once we hit puberty. From then on, we spend most of our time in generative relationships—whether seeking one, recovering from one, or mourning one. All along the way webs of friendships, congregations, clubs, and colleagues sustain us. We may say we are lonely along the way, but hardly ever solitary. Indeed, much of our distress signals how very social we are. Much of what we count as pain, shame and struggle are an insatiable, if sometimes inept, search for vital relationships. We need each other.

While it is obvious that human relationships are quite a trick to sustain, the only life we will ever know is social. We create families because that is the only way we live. We create neighborhoods, cities, nations, and other global things for the same reason. We can't help it. That's just the way humans live. We have zero capacity to stay apart, and do not know how not to relate. The Chinese built a wall to isolate themselves, but over time it became useless. Bhutan was defined by its isolation from the culture-changing influences from India and the West. One of the cracks in this isolationism came from a persistent Norwegian medical missionary family who offered to open a small hospital on the border to provide modern services otherwise unavailable in the kingdom. The king eventually decided that the exposure to the West necessary in order to bring the Norwegian hospital inside the borders was less corrosive than forcing his citizens to travel outside Bhutan to find medical care. This complex calculation makes the point: even the king of Bhutan had to manage his relationship with the West, not just defend his separation.

We just can't stay apart even when we most desperately want to, even when we have no clue about how to be together. We can't help it. Human life works really well and is capable of astonishing resilience and recovery.

—m—

When Larry and I began to interview people about the Leading Causes of Life, we wanted to see how the words *connection*, *coherence*, *agency*, *blessing*, and *hope* surfaced in the lives of individuals at the Center for Hope and Healing in Memphis. The Center for Hope and Healing is a ministry of the Church Health Center that has powerfully harnessed the compassion and energy of both churches and the medical community in Memphis to provide medical care for those who would otherwise be left out of the system. The Center for Hope and Healing—with its gym, nutrition classes, programs for children, and emphasis on healthy lifestyle—looks a great deal like a YMCA. Ella Weddington, a volunteer and member of the Church Health Center, was Larry's first interview. Not surprisingly, our interview couldn't help but wonder about cause.

"Do you think this facility could be called the Center for Healing and Hope?" Larry asked her. Did healing cause hope? Or did hope cause healing? It took her just a moment to answer.

"It has to be Hope and Healing," she said. "Hope has to be there first. Hope is something you look forward to and once you get to a certain point then the healing takes place almost automatically. So I'd say the enemy of healing is despair. I'd also say that hope is just 'there.' We don't create it."

For Ella hope is the cause, and healing the result.

For Larry life was the cause, and hope the result.

The events of November 13, 2003, caused my life to change. For several days cells in my brain had been dying. One by one, then hundreds by hundreds, then millions by millions my neurons fell like leaves swept from an autumn tree. Suddenly clocks made no sense to me. "Yes, that's a clock," I said to myself. But I had no idea how to tell the time. Neither could I speak in a voice that sounded even vaguely familiar.

"How are you, Dad?" my children asked.

"I'm fine, but I'm not me," I answered.

Several months later I entered the Headway rehabilitation program at St. Vincent's Hospital. Rehabilitation, I soon discovered, isn't about a cure. Instead it is all about life. Our group was always changing as people cycled in and out of rehabilitation and as new patients arrived. When we met together, we would often introduce ourselves by sharing what happened when the car crashed, when the rope broke, when the horse fell, when a clot caused our cells to be swept away, or our brain began to leak. Cause, for us, was easy to find. The MRIs and CAT scans pinpointed with scientific certainty exactly why we mispronounced words, could not make sense of a clock, follow directions, or move the way we had once moved.

But applying cause to life—that was a different matter. How would we ever heal when the events that took our lives away could not be undone nor their consequences taken away? For life to return we had to practice the mechanics of subtraction that we thought we had forever learned in second grade. We had to learn once again how to follow directions and how to understand the sequence in solving even the simplest of problems. Speech therapy, physical therapy, occupational therapy, recreational therapy all became the hardest work of my life as neurons that had never been used to subtract learned to subtract, as voice slowly rediscovered it had not been slain in the trauma of brain injury.

When the patients gathered for the weekly "Head Ed" class, the conversation inevitably drifted into a reconnoitering of the strange new world in which we found ourselves. I realized, that the hard work of rehabilitation was not designed to return us to the life we once knew. Instead, it was all about creating, finding and affirming a new life. By this point, Gary and I had been working on the Leading Causes of Life for some time. One by one, distilled and clarified by the very injuries that swept away so much of my life, the five Leading Causes presented themselves.

My therapists were adamant about connection. They made it clear that the active support of friends, family, and community are necessary if life is to gain a new foothold. Without them the road ahead will be made more difficult than it already is. Healing should not be a lonely experience. When family and friends were not involved, the rehab staff went out of their way to provide a sustaining connection.

They told me that reestablishing life would be the hardest work I had ever done in my life. They didn't use the word agency, but the expectations were clear. I would have to show up, and keep showing up. I would have to work through anger and despair. When I couldn't solve a problem I would have to try it again, and then again, and then still again.

Like the other patients, I had to create a new world of meaning that built on the past but didn't replicate it. What made sense in the past would not suffice for the future. In fact, for all of us, comparison became the archenemy as it opened the door to despair. Call it purpose or call it coherence, something new had to take root. Life, just life, not status, not employment, not titles, not denial, not false hope—*life* had to begin again.

"Time is on your side," the therapists said to those of us in the group. The swelling, the seizures, the overwhelming exhaustion, will all slowly pass away. Slowly motion will return or compensations will be found. In the days of rebirth when it seems like nothing is happening, time is on your side. These words filled us with incredible hope. None of us knew what the future held, but time itself was on our side.

And blessing? Could there be blessing when so much is taken away? Could there be blessing in the fights with insurance companies? It is amazing how often patients in rehabilitation find themselves saying, and perhaps believing, that their accident brought about a reordering of life's priorities. Sometimes we said this just to keep hope alive; sometimes we said it to keep depression at bay. Not one of us would have chosen the trauma we experienced. But in its traumatic wake we learned something about life that we might not have otherwise experienced.

During the long months of rehab, all we could do was practice life. To have simply heard the words "you will live" without ways to harness that which causes life would not have been enough. Causality is both as concrete as an automobile accident, as a fall off a horse, or as a clot in the brain that says to blood, "this far, and no farther," and as mysterious as the re-creation of life itself.

Larry

People think that rehabilitation is about recovery. But Larry knows differently. Rehabilitation, he says, is the creation of a new life.

> Our world is in need of rehabilitation that brings about connections deep enough to harness life, a shared sense of values known as cohesion, blessing capable of rearranging our priorities in ways that emphasize life, and hope strong enough to transcend circumstance.

Why does that story of Larry's rehabilitation story matter? It matters because our world is in need of rehabilitation that brings about connections deep enough to harness life, a shared sense of values known as cohesion, blessing capable of rearranging our priorities in ways that emphasize life, and hope strong enough to transcend circumstance. In short, we have causes that both teach us much about life and flow from life's very essence.

Sociologist Aaron Antonovsky's own life was turned around when he noticed that 29 percent of women who had endured Nazi death camps (not to mention three wars in Israel in the space of 15 years) described themselves as being in good emotional health. This was compared to 51 percent of the control group of women who had not endured these bitter ordeals.[25] Most sociologists would want to know why only 51 percent of women thought their mental health good; but Antonovsky was mystified by the 29 percent who had "gone through the most unimaginable horror of the camp, followed by years of being a displaced person, and then to have reestablished one's life in a country which witnessed three wars . . . and still be in reasonable health."[26] Zero health would have been a more likely guess for a group like that.

How could Antonovsky explain the positive health of such a battered and scarred group of women? Antonovsky theorized that the women's mysterious contentment derived from the fact that they had a way of understanding the suffering that made their lives somewhat coherent and, to a degree, predictable. Like many violated persons throughout history, these women saw their suffering as part of a multi-generation arc of cultural history. This made their lives not only bearable, but even noble. They could understand themselves and their suffering.

Antonovsky spent the last years of his life fascinated by just that mystery, the same one

Life is the fundamental mystery, not death.

that compels us long after his death. He located this mystery in the heart of what he called "coherence." Antonovsky's definition of coherence is a little bit broader than my definition. Antonovsky found coherence to be so crucial for humans that he loaded the one word with at least three of our Leading Causes of Life: coherence, agency, and blessing. His basic point is that *life* is the fundamental mystery, not death. Where does all this life come from? How it is sustained? How can I align my own life with life? For those answers we turn to the five Leading Causes of Life: connection, coherence, agency, blessing, and hope.

—m—

The Five Causes

The World Wide Web is not just a communication device, but a powerful agent of change.

Tom Munnecke, a software designer, philosopher, social entrepreneur, and friend of mine, believes that "transformational ensembles" can change the world. More precisely, he thinks they are what are *already* changing it, if we know how to recognize them. "Transformational ensembles" is the delightful language he uses to describe the minimum set of factors capable of sustaining transformation.[27] The World Wide Web is an example of this amazingly successful process. The Web's ensemble is very simple: just a few basic rules of how to code information so that connected computers can find each other and share information across these connections. The ensemble doesn't make the connections; it only makes them possible, which makes them useful and therefore extremely valuable, especially to humans whose life thrives across complex connections. What looks like a technical, mechanical phenomenon is really a life process, an example of human life finding its way toward a higher level of complexity. The Web is so successful that the transformation has touched almost every aspect of communication, learning, and organizing across the planet. Habitat for Humanity is an organizational example of a simple transformational ensemble using hammers rather than electrons. Habitat for Humanity is nothing more than an ensemble of rules: no interest charged, sweat equity by the new owner, and local volunteers—over and over and over. And it works. Habitat is well on its way to building its two millionth home.[28]

The Leading Causes of Life are a simple ensemble that makes possible the miracle of sustained human life—over and over and over. Let's start with *connection*.

CHAPTER THREE
Connection

Humans are social creatures. Capable of only brief episodes of solitude, human life thrives on our social connections to each other. In fact, human life is *only* found in the extraordinary number of connections humans make with their families, friends, neighbors, faith members, and fellow citizens. Connections are like the breath of air on which our very lives depend.

I was finishing my morning workout on September 11, 2001, when I heard the report of an airplane crash on Yellowstone Public Radio. Within a moment or two it was clear the news bulletin was becoming a story. Downstairs, Jim and Jayanthi Wilson, missionaries from Lesotho, heard something was happening and tuned in to the television. It was clear the day's ministries would change. Jim and Jayanthi headed for Buffalo, Wyoming, knowing their talk with a church would be far more than a mission report. I headed over to church and immediately called all of our deacons, asking them to come over to the church as soon as they could. As they arrived, we began to ponder the essential questions of mission: What good can be done? And by what means?

It didn't take long to come up with a plan of action. We decided to call every member of our small congregation to see how they were doing, to share with them that the church would be open all day, and that we were organizing a community service that would be held that night. We would devote the day to the ministry of connection. We quickly divided up the church directory, and began to make the calls. We made posters announcing the service and distributed them in the windows of all the stores on Main Street. All day long people stopped by the church. They too were checking in, touching base, affirming life through the gift of connection.[29]

Our hundred or so calls in Big Timber, Montana, were an almost infinitesimally small proportion of the billions of calls made that day as the nation and the world responded to death by affirming the connections that sustain life.

Larry

—⚬—

Our minds seem to be designed for the task of recognizing, initiating, managing, and responding to this dense fabric of highly complex social relationships. Human language hides much of this complexity by neatly sorting us all into broad categories: man, woman, husband, wife, brother, sister, cousin (of multiple orders), uncle, aunt, neighbor, member, citizen. We have long lists of simple names for very complex relationships. However, the brain is capable of much finer feats of recognition, and much more subtle variations among these connections. Recently, 51 members of the Gunderson clan gathered in the mountains of Tennessee. On the drive, we studied the list of family members, explaining to our daughter the permutations of relationships that accumulate over four generations (three present in the flesh, and Mom and Dad very present in a different way). We are capable of *being* in more complex relationships than we have words for.

Scientists with time on their hands have figured out that the human brain can recognize the face of someone it has met among thousands of non-familiar faces in less than a quarter of a second.[30] This is not the face of someone they've had sex with, mind you; just someone they've seen before. That's a brain designed for human connection.

Connection is so deeply woven into the fabric of reality that Greg Fricchione traces it back to the Big Bang. Greg is head of psychiatry at Women's and Children's Hospitals at Harvard University, where he sees patients at a time of profound vulnerability, despair, and even dread. He reads human experience, and all of life, as a tension between attachment (what I call *connection*) and separation.[31] He sees the evolution of pre-biotic life, to animal life, to humans as a fundamental cycle in which we face the basic challenges of survival. The most basic task of any life form is to decide if it should move toward or away from something. "Do I need to separate or attach?" The questions get more complicated as we evolve, of course, as we have more complicated needs and more subtle threats. Early single-cell creatures faced basic problems of finding enough energy, and were pretty lethargic and vulnerable as a result. These little biomachines were separated from sources of food that would give them energy. At some point in the dim past, some of them figured out how to entice mitochondria to live inside their cell walls. This attachment strategy worked so well that the two of them became inseparable, (every one of the billions of cells in your body is still doing this, and you might want to stop reading and thank them).

The point Fricchione makes is that this kind of separation challenge, which was answered by a more complex connection strategy, has been the ongoing pattern that has continued through all organic life. He finds the pattern in the structural evolution of the human brain, which differs from "lower animals" primarily by its (our) structural capacity to manage more and more complex social relationships. We are built for connection and biased to respond to basic survival challenges by developing more complex connections. The apparently insurmountable challenge of global warming appears

We are built for connection and biased to respond to basic survival challenges by developing more complex connections.

likely to separate us from the climate we need in order to live. I'd guess that Fricchione would bet that the human strategy likely to emerge will be a highly complex connection that will permit us to manage our global behavior and bend the curve of global warming into something we can live with. Our current level of connection won't do it, so we need to evolve a new level of connection. For that purpose we have memory and, more interestingly, anticipation.

Humans have very long memories. Memory is a powerful tool of attachment since it allows those of us with a memory (including me, on good days) to go back to those things that have given us life in the past. That may be remembering something that made you happy, or something that taught you a lesson. It might just be re-membering where I left my keys, without which I could not keep my job and have food to eat. Memory helps. We also remember the lives of helpful people, such as Archbishop Desmond Tutu, who re-minds us of the pathway of faith, courage, and love that attaches us and gives us life.

Humans don't just remember; we anticipate. As a psychiatrist, Fricchione sees the upside and downside of a unique human charac-teristic: we know that we all face an ultimate separation from those that have given us life and love. This dread drives us to form deeper, more complex relationships that we hope will survive after we die. The human ability to look ahead toward the future is as powerful as memory; it shapes our choices to achieve connections that might give us life. We remember the future, and we express our agency (capac-ity to do) in ways that make that future happen. Recognizing a pos-sible future with enough clarity to move toward it is a highly sophisticated capacity. We think it is natural to imagine things that are not yet present, to hope for things that might be, and to act on those hopes. Sometimes this feels like it is inside our heads, but Fricchione would recognize that it is precisely the opposite. We are able to sketch a future only as a way of finding more life amid the connections that give us life already. We try to remember our way into a future be-cause we are connected to those relationships that are alive for us.

Connection, for humans, drives our unique characteristics including religion, which means "to bind back," to connect. Fricchione says, "Spirituality emerges in our contemplation of the 'pining emotion' we orphans feel, separated as we are from our Parent. As creatures experiencing the pain of separation, we seek healing in being bound back through authentic religion."[32] This ultimate separation crisis drives the ultimate connection solution through selfless love toward others and a spiritual experience of connection to the ultimate source of all life itself.

—⚹—

It was easy to find a starting point for a conversation about life with Dr. David Wright, MD. Larry interviewed him on a Saturday morning at the Church Health Center in Memphis. David is one of the 400 or so physicians who volunteer their time at the Church Health Center on a regular basis to see patients who, without their services, might have no doctor at all. It seems only natural that his story is one that illuminates connection. In the medical world, it often goes without saying that many medical appointments are fraught with fear. If something weren't "wrong" there would be no reason for the appointment. Fear leads to loneliness and loneliness tends to make one vulnerable to disease.

Fear leads to loneliness and loneliness tends to make one vulnerable to disease.

"I think most encounters in the medical system tend to be lonely," said David. "You wait in this cubical, and are then told to go to another room. It feels like nobody knows your name, and then even your clothes, a sign of who you are, are taken away. Loneliness damages you in such a core way that you end up not really caring about yourself or anybody else. It is the very opposite of Jesus' command that we are to 'Love the Lord your God . . . and love your neighbor as yourself.'"

Knowing how important connection is in the healing process, David has learned to assess it as part of each exam.

"You certainly get a feel for loneliness or connection from the tone of the conversation with patients, even if they don't name it

Patients who are connected survive medical setbacks that would shatter those who are isolated and lonely. Connection has healing power. specifically," he said. "When I ask them, 'Tell me about your family,' and they respond by saying, 'Well my dad lived to an old age, but I don't know what he died of,' that indicates one thing. If they say, 'Oh, let me tell you about my granddaughter,' that tells something else. The other way to discern it is to see if a family member comes for them when they are seriously ill."

For David, healing happens best when it is dense with connections—patient and physician, patient and congregation or friends and family, patient with self and patient with God. Patients who are connected survive medical setbacks that would shatter those who are isolated and lonely.

Connection has healing power.

—⚇—

Communities could use some of that healing power. The Interfaith Health Program (IHP) trains teams of community leaders in a program developed with the Centers for Disease Control and Prevention.[33] The curriculum is based on the concept of "boundary leadership," which is basically the art of leadership that is useful in the in-between spaces of community. Many see communities as broken and sick; we see them as capable of being connected in new ways that allow them to live. Boundary leadership works in the rich spaces of ambiguous control where most everything that matters happens.[34] In-between space isn't dying—it's life finding a way. That in-between space—think back to Henry Turley's Uptown neighborhood—is not empty just because it's not in anyone's control. It is filled with relationships, just like the radio waves that fill the air even up here in the mountains where I am typing at this moment. Most

Many see communities as broken and sick; we see them as capable of being connected in new ways that allow them to live. In-between space isn't dying—it's life finding a way.

70

professionals are not trained for the boundary zones. They are trained for institutional spaces where we learn about hierarchy, discipline, order, and rules of engagement. It takes about 18 years of formal education to learn those odd arts, but over time we come to think of them as what is "normal." We are taught to see boundary zones as being untamed (they are) and unnatural (they aren't). We become like lions raised in the zoo, which have forgotten who we are and what we are good for. Boundary zones are where perspective-changing, idea-changing, and life-changing connections actually happen. We can't forget to seek out these connections.

—∿—

A couple of years ago, my family and I were in South Africa in Kreuger Park where the lions are free, and the humans are confined in little metal boxes called cars that roll around the landscape. One morning we caught word that a ranger had killed a giraffe which had broken its leg, and that a pride of lions was preparing for lunch. We drove out across the veldt to find another 20 cars surrounding the scene. It turned out that two male lions were negotiating over the giraffe, and taking their time about it, much to the disgust of the females of the pride. Shortly after we pulled up, the lionesses decided they'd had enough waiting, and went to go find some zebra to snack on while the main giraffe course was prepared. We had not noticed a herd of zebra a hundred yards off to the north, but the lionesses did. The pride walked right by our car—their heads not six inches from where my apparently unappetizing bottom had been sticking out of the window moments before. As they moved from the road into the grass, they went into the elaborate social pattern in which lions hunt. The oldest took the center, with another one guarding her back by keeping a discreet gaze on the idiot humans in the cars (you just never know what humans will do). The younger lionesses spread off in a deliberate quarter mile arc through the tall winter grass up and beyond the zebra. They disappeared, of course, as their coats were indistinguishable from the color of the grass, and their smooth pace blended with the ebb and flow of the breeze. The lions were perfect in every way because they were perfectly adapted. The zebra are also perfectly adapted, so it would take hours for the lunchtime drama to play out.

When I returned to the United States I told this story to Fred Smith, a friend, theologian, and pastor who helped develop the IHP Institute. He asked me a question that has never left me, "Gary, for what are *we* perfectly adapted?" What is the environment in which we could be as totally fit as a lion in the tall winter grass of Africa? Giraffes are fit for the trees. Ostriches (an animal that proves God's sense of humor) are fit for the savanna. So are iguanas fit for the Galapagos Islands. That is exactly what caught Darwin's curiosity, and drove a revolution in understanding life. For what are we perfectly adapted?

The answer is that we are adapted for complex social relationships. We are adapted for connection relevant to the work of transforming the communities we love. The complex connections we find in all the in-between spaces of our broken cities come as naturally to humans as hunting to a lion. This is very convenient because connections cause our sustained life.

Every mammal mates in order to bear live young. Humans do too, for which I am grateful beyond my capacity to say. Humans go far beyond other mammals because of our rich complexity of social relationships. In *Deeply Woven Roots*, I explore the social strengths of congregations. One of these strengths is a congregation's capacity to connect people beyond the lines of blood and money.[35] Congregations generate health and wholeness because of how they connect people. Congregations did this long before we even had printing presses, and will do so long after the cell phones go dead, because congregations are social spaces in which people can connect to each other. They gradually come to know the multi-layered, many-faceted breadth of each other. As time goes by, those layers and facets gain more depth and resonance, allowing more kinds of connection. Not always and not smoothly, of course. They can also sustain disconnection by promoting and sustaining myths of

> We are adapted for complex social relationships. We are adapted for connection relevant to the work of transforming the communities we love. Connections cause our sustained life.

separation, difference, and danger. But there is a reason that every sustained human culture has some kind of social network that is recognizable as a type of congregation. It is a life form that you'd expect to find wherever you find humans.

Families are perhaps even more fundamental connections. Beyond bread, water, shelter, and occasional fresh sperm, families connect their members to the stuff of human life. We find the mysteries of kindness, tenderness, play, and delight. We find encouragement, modeling of purpose and sacrifice, and the memory of those before us. The complex dynamics of families prepare us for the endless complexities of other vital connections. In a living family, all of these connections generate the qualities of sustained human life, and they do this not just because they enable stability. It is quite the reverse. They enable adaptivity, resilience, and innovation. Adaptivity sustains life, and we learn adaptivity from our most intimate connections in the family.

> Congregations generate health and wholeness because of how they connect people. Congregations did this long before we even had printing presses, and will do so long after the cell phones go dead, because congregations are social spaces in which people can connect to each other.

In the United States these days, we are having the most remarkably silly arguments over the definition of a family—as if rules could apply in this most mysteriously generative space. The number crunchers among us have noted that roughly 24.1 percent of current "families" are composed of ensembles including one wife and one husband married only to each other, and having children born only to them.[36] The rest of the spectrum of family connections almost defies attempts at categorization. I would not even try. The vocabulary of our times hints at the tapestry now found in almost all neighborhoods: mixed, blended, and adoptive families led by life partners. We fumble at parties introducing each other, trying to find simple labels for complicated relationships. Fortunately, we are perfectly adapted for such confusion and find our way.

73

Human life is caused by our connectedness. The more connected we are, the more generative, adaptive, and complex our life is likely to be. There is a balance to be had, of course, but humans clearly find sustenance in complex relationships. It comes naturally to us. It is what we are perfectly adapted for. Families are complicated enough. "Blended families" are an order of magnitude beyond them. The thing to notice is that humans are capable of managing quite well in such complexity. Even the most rigidly conservative evangelical churches have a riot of complexity going on that they have no language to describe. Indeed, the health of the human enterprise depends on complex connections.

> **Human life is caused by our connectedness. The more connected we are, the more generative, adaptive, and complex our life is likely to be.**

—ɯ—

The Africa Religious Health Assets Program (ARHAP) is a mélange of academics and activists based mostly in Southern Africa (with partners in Memphis, Norway, and Germany).[37] We came together out of our shared need to understand how religion on the ground in Africa is an asset for the health of the community. We were driven, of course, by the urgent scale and scope of the AIDS catastrophe. Until scientists figured out how the virus spreads, and how it does not, it was reasonable to be afraid. But we've understood the basics of HIV/AIDS for many years now, so fear is not the only reasonable approach. Once the basics were clear, further detail of the pathology didn't help a great deal. We probably understand more about the virus' way of life than we do about our own. As the virus undermined entire societies, it was critical to understand not just what was wrong, but what we had to work with.

The irony was that AIDS traveled perfectly across our most intimate connections, turning them from a pathway of life to a path of death. The virus understood how to take advantage of our hypocrisies about those connections, especially about the reliable patterns of power, gender, and culture. This is a social disease that turns our complex connections against us.

AHRAP needed to understand our connections—including our religious ones—in a deeper way so that we could bend them toward life. It seems that humanity has always contended with some sort of disease that is so dreadful that we fear those infected even more than the infection itself. So it was with leprosy. We created colonies apart for the lepers, forcing those victims who might come near us to wear bells so we could hear and avoid them. Today, long after our ignorance should have been dispelled, we treat those infected with HIV in ways that any 14th-century leper would recognize. Somehow, we allowed ourselves to become dumber than a gaggle of single-celled creatures.

We decided to do some basic research about how faith and health were understood in the small, land-locked Southern African nation of Lesotho. I could say that we chose Lesotho because of its screamingly high HIV infection rate (about 40 percent of childbearing-age women).[38] Actually, we had good connections: one of our faculty, Paul Germond, was there, having descended from four generations of French missionaries. His terrifically smart students paved the way. We developed a nice questionnaire to guide this research that centered on discussing connecting faith and health. This quickly ran into trouble when we learned over a cell phone call from Sepetla Molapo, a Sesotho graduate student, that his language had no words that separated faith from health. The whole point of our research was how to connect faith and health, and it turned out that they are not separate. You can't connect what is not separate—and our Sesotho friends thought that we were a bit dim to even ask. Instead of our Western eyes that look for mechanically separate body parts, the Sesotho have a unified concept called *Bophelo*. We are primed to see things as separate; they can see the integral reality.

The good news is that when human connections fail, a host of other connections pick up the slack. Larry recounts that the depth of the word *Bophelo* became clear to him when he interviewed Sepetla for this book:

Sepetla: "When we started out, we went to the villages and asked what their religious health assets were."

Larry: "And what did they say?"

Sepetla: "They said 'the mountains.'" There was both glee and wonderment in his voice. The mountains are the source of Lesotho's water, a place of safety, symbols of things that do not change. To live in Lesotho, which is known as the Mountain Kingdom, without an awareness of the mountains would be strange indeed.

"And then they said 'the rivers.' Then they said, 'the roads which bring us together, allowing us to visit other villages and our relatives, which bring goods to us.' And then they said, 'the fields which grow our food.'"

Sepetla went on to report the villagers gave thanks for the doctors and nurses, for whatever health care there might be; but it all had to be part of a whole. In other words, if you heal in a small town like Morija then everything around you—a doctor, a small hospital, healers, mountains, roads, rivers, and fields—would all be on your side, each one part of a healing connection that called on each part of life. And, of course, what is true of the beautiful Morija is true of Big Timber, or Memphis.

—⁓—

Bophelo, the Sesotho word for wholeness, is a way of talking about the health of the whole connected ensemble—a person inseparable from a family, which is inseparable from community, which is inseparable from "the people," who are inseparable from the land and creation.[39] To even describe it as "connected" implies that it could be separated. A diamond has facets, not parts. A community has dimensions, not parts. Within *Bophelo*, any separation is a fissure in the life of every facet of the whole. Our Sesotho colleagues learned that *Bophelo* "is constituted of a complex web of social relationships which are, themselves, the source of *Bophelo*; and *Bophelo* is fundamentally based on trust."[40] A violation of this trust is every bit as deadly as a virus, if not more so.

You'd think they'd need a big chart to keep all these highly complex relationships straightened out, but they don't. Indeed, our desire to chart and name it amused them. They understood that sustained human life is an expression of the whole. It is accurate to say that human life is *caused* by those connections—all of them, all of the time. These days, connections in Lesotho are torn, tattered, and scattered in a thousand ways. AIDS is only one opportunistic infection in the body of the whole, distinctive only because of its relatively short-term consequences. The wise people of Lesotho know that AIDS is dealt with only in the context of the *Bophelo* of the whole. This is frustrating to the Western experts who have such effective pills and machines, but no apparent *Bophelo* of their own to share. Africans have seen American and European TV and know that our doctors deserve some sympathy because of the difficulties of finding health in such vacant, disconnected communities. It is a fair question: should you trust pills that come from people who obviously know little about wholeness?

The insidious power of AIDS is in out-adapting the human carrier. Healthy generative human communities are connected in ways that enable them to adapt to changing threats and opportunities as a whole. Unhealthy human communities find themselves incapable of adapting to reality because their connections are no longer generative and complex. To be healthy, communities must talk to each other about sex, gender, family, poverty, wealth, privilege, meaning, and power. Unhealthy communities' equally insidious, fear-filled brittleness toward connectedness makes all that nearly impossible. They are broken, linked only on the surface, and thus highly vulnerable to a virus smart enough to exploit their discontinuities and hypocrisies.

Outside experts come from the very organizations and governments that had a role in undermining local culture and politics. The fracture of community breaks *Bophelo*, which is the whole problem creating the need for medical help. Four generations after French and British missionaries brought medicine, education, and external power to Lesotho, French, and British organizations still provide a substantial portion of the medical resources to a people who remain stunningly enmeshed in poverty.

Essentially, expertise in antiretroviral therapy (ART) comes from the same kind of universities that teach the mining technology that lure away the men of Lesotho by the thousands, destroying their families in the process. I think of Wendell Berry who observes that universities tend to think that those who create knowledge have little responsibility for the eventual uses of that knowledge. Knowledge, like other forms of power, tends to be most useful to those who already have a lot of power. The mine owners, not the mineworkers, tend to gain the most from university geology and engineering departments. So, it is not surprising that the poor of Lesotho would tend to expect that those coming with new medical knowledge would tend to serve those institutions that benefit the established order of society, not them. This is especially true when the medical experts seem to be so lacking in any apparent *Bophelo*.

> It is understandable that a person in Lesotho would cautiously regard a medical technician who seems highly skilled at fighting an invisible virus, but is too dull to notice all else that gives life.

The medicine "works" as much as it prolongs one person's life, but it cannot restore *Bophelo*. It doesn't even know it is there to be broken. Normal Western medical science isn't smart enough to see what's missing, because its theory has already stripped it out of sight. Any Lesotho adult notices that most Western medicine only sees a very small slice of human experience.

What difference would such sensitivity make for managing a disease anyway? Simple villagers might not know anything about the particular virus called HIV, but they would know that persons' resistance to almost any other kind of disease depends on their relationships. Health isn't just about invisible bugs; it is about connecting to loved ones, to the village that gives one life, and to the natural order that is one's breath and hope. It is understandable that a person in Lesotho would cautiously regard a medical technician who seems highly skilled at fighting an invisible virus, but is too dull to notice all else that gives life.

Mainstream medicine barely shows any consciousness of consciousness, much less of family dynamics, much less of the full community. But even *American* scientists could see *Bophelo* if they knew to look for it. We would have to start looking for rich connectedness as a causal root of healthy sustained

> It is a much smarter way to see the world: as a thick weave of relationships, every one of which plays more than a single functional role in sustaining life.

human communities and the individuals who live in them. That demands a richer theory of life with more happening in and around human communities than just bugs and diseases. We want to receive medicine from someone who seems to understand life, not just death.

Life comes, and is sustained, through our connections. It is a much smarter way to see the world: as a thick weave of relationships, every one of which plays more than a single functional role in sustaining life. This confounds the simple Western mind, which likes the brother to stay only a brother and not be a lender, a boss, a teacher, or a shaman. "Keep the roles separate," we say. "One role for each function," we say. That is simply not the way of sustained humanity.

—⁄Ⱳ—

Down the block from Henry Turley's Uptown office is Roxie's. Roxie's looks like a dumpy, code-violating corner store and grill that any public health officer would recognize as a risk vector (a "risk vector" is a public health term that connotes the pathway along which a risk can develop into a disease or injury). Roxie's, on the other hand, is actually a *life* vector—a connecting point for many kinds of relationships, across which sizzle vital stuff like food, hope, and intelligence. It is a multi-relevant connection, just the kind that humans prefer. These types of connection can be generative community centers, churches capable of giving life, or even, as Henry dearly hopes, a realtor's office.

Connections give more life as they connect more people in more ways. To call such capacity "bandwidth" imports an internet metaphor that limits the idea of life, but it at least points the mind toward highly connected relationships. The better language is the language of life. When we start using words like *Bophelo*, we can really begin to talk about the dense weave of layered relationships in which our lives connect.

Connection is vital, but insufficient. If you only see connections, you'd have a start, but you'd soon find yourself noticing what is happening among and within those relationships. That's the way life works. The logic of the Leading Causes of Life is that any one of the causes will generate the space for the others to express themselves and flourish into a full ensemble. Roxie's doesn't stay just a store. It wants to be a spring of coherence (belonging and finding meaning), a source of agency (capacity to do), a web of blessing, and a front for hope. It's a lot to ask of a store, but life makes it so.

It is the combination of the Leading Causes of Life that makes sustainable, vital, and generative life possible. You certainly can have just one cause of life, but if you don't have the others the life probably won't last very long.

Connection is vital, but insufficient. If you only see connections, you'd have a start, but you'd soon find yourself noticing what is happening among and within those relationships. That's the way life works. The logic of the Leading Causes of Life is that any one of the causes will generate the space for the others to express themselves and flourish into a full ensemble.

It is important to note that prisoners have connection but little life because they have so little of the other causes of life. What environment could be less coherent (a sense of belonging and meaning), offering such constrained agency (capacity to do), so distant from hope? The movie *The Shawshank Redemption* told a story of crushing confinement redeemed only through a struggle to preserve the coherence, agency, and hope of the main character, Andy.[41]

There are few such stories in the medieval-type jails holding a significant fraction of young men of color today. Viktor Frankl noticed that the prisoners in Nazi camps survived if they had hope, not just the connections that bound them into a terribly confined community.[42] Connection confined is like a seed trying to grow on a Wal-Mart parking lot. Sometimes the seed does break through to the soil below, but usually not.

But back to Roxie's. If you know how life works, you'll see that Roxie's is alive. Like an individual, life will connect in ever more complex ways, eventually losing its sense of autonomy and separation from its neighborhood. This is why Roxie's may be a more vital source of life in this neighborhood than most of the churches. Its doors are open for many more hours, and the standards for entry are much lower. More types of people with more complex lives come in and out, and they are probably more naturally comfortable with each other than they might be dressed up in church. This is also why Roxie's is more useful to the community than a chain grocery store might be. Roxie's life depends on its neighbors' trust, its web of connections, and its deep knowledge of its patrons. A chain grocery store with a location near my home depends on some office in Cincinnati and a business plan built on replication, not organic connection. I tend to shop in this store because I'm new in town and I know what to expect there. It fits my disconnected transient self, which anyone in Lesotho would know is not healthy.

So how do we connect? Sometimes it's with people. And sometimes, especially when fear has pervaded the life of a people, it is a matter of aesthetics. On his trips to Russia and Romania to report on the mission work of the Russian and Romanian Orthodox Churches, Larry couldn't help but find the drab Stalinist or community architecture to be an affront to the soul. Building doors were invariably ugly, apartment buildings invariably utilitarian in the worst sense of the word. But within these structures were symbols of life: an icon, a painting, a geranium, each representing hope. And there were the stunning doors of churches that had somehow survived an ideology that did its best to disconnect people from God or the spiritual life. These doors were green, blue, yellow, or gold, each sending an invitation saying, "These are the doors that lead to life." Inside the churches, the paintings of saints seemed to say, "You are not alone." The golden domes of cathedrals reflected not just light, but the hoped-for light of the soul as well. Their beauty gave hope to a faith that had to be nurtured privately or even secretly. Sometimes connection depends on people; and sometimes it is equally powerful when a person connects with an idea, a symbol, a sustaining hope.

> **How do we connect? Sometimes it's with people. And sometimes, especially when fear has pervaded the life of a people, it is a matter of aesthetics.**

—∞—

It didn't take long for me to learn that James Fisher has an alias at the Center for Hope and Healing in Memphis. Everyone calls him

Fish. If you go to the gym, with its rows of gleaming weight machines, and ask about Fish everyone will know who you mean. If you arrive at the Center's door at six in the morning, chances are Fish will greet you there. Fish isn't a staff member. He doesn't show up at the Center because he has to. He shows up because it would feel odd not to.

"I'm here six days a week," he said. "Some days I exercise, and some days I run my mouth," he adds with a smile. Then he deepens the observation. Aimless talk isn't why he arrives early. It is talk about people's lives that counts. It is talk that says, "you matter." It is talk that connects people; talk that provides both blessing and hope.

"There are people here who need a conversation, so you take time and have a conversation with them," he said. "A lot of people come here with the weight of the world on their shoulders, and you can see it on their faces. I'll go up to them and ask, 'What is it about today? Do you want to talk about it?' And they'll say, 'Yes.' It may be problems at home or problems with their grandchildren."

"It must mean a lot to people when you ask them how they're doing," Larry said to him during an interview. The words were no sooner out of Larry's mouth than he pointed Larry in another direction.

"Well, you know," he said, "I never did like that idea of asking, 'How are you doing?' It has a tendency to make a person feel weak. So now I prefer to ask, 'What's up? What are we going to do today? Doing anything today?' I find some way to approach them other than asking, 'How are you feeling?'"

Fish's way of starting a conversation zeros in on life and cares about how people are responding to despair, loneliness, or helplessness. His questions are active, not passive. The conversations that ensue don't have a heavy feeling to them because they reflect a community where connection matters.

"There's a lot of interest in people's whole lives here," he said. "To me, we are more or less a family that reaches out to other families and individuals. Conversations aren't pushed away. People expect conversations when they are here. I know they expect a conversation out of me.

"If I go over to the Church Health Center where people are waiting to see a doctor," he said, "and I see somebody I know, I'll say,

'What's up today? What are you going to do when you leave here?' Or I'll say, 'When you leave here have a blessed day. Be careful, and have a blessed day.'"

"What do you mean by 'Be careful'?" Larry asked.

"I mean, don't do anything God wouldn't approve of your doing," he said, "Don't go in the store and say, 'Well, these two bags of potato chips are packaged together so I guess I'll get them both instead of getting just one.' You know. Be mindful of what God would have you do."

It is not surprising that Fish knows a lot of people at the Center for Hope and Healing. When he became a mentor, he was assigned 43 people to call each week for two years. He would ask if they had been taking their medications, if they were exercising, if they were minding their diet and testing their blood sugars. His calls became an extension of the doctor's office. From a medical point of view his calls were crucial. They had the power to prevent the life-threatening complications of obesity or diabetes. Most patients with chronic diseases leave the doctor's office knowing what they *should* do, but find it far easier said than done. Just as it is easier to keep a New Year's resolution when it is shared with another person, so Fish's calls served as a follow-up and as a call to accountability. The connections Fish so skillfully established would point the way to life for many of those he called.

—⁂—

Like most pastors, Larry loves a wedding. When a couple asks him to marry them he gives an encouraging word and then arranges times to meet with them over the coming months. In the course of their meetings he invariably says these words: "There are no words one human being can say to another that are more powerful, more life changing, than, 'I love you and will spend the rest of my life with you.' The two of you have no idea what lies ahead of you. But you do know this: Whatever life brings, you will face it and share it together."

He reminds them—and us—that vows are the words of connection that do indeed steer us through life. They have the power to shape lives that cannot be held hostage to circumstance. It doesn't

> **Connection is the powerful and ever-changing concoction of people, things, and beliefs that matter. Humans cannot predict its impact. That lies in the province of blessing. But human beings can go out of their way to find and embrace it.**

take long, for every couple discovers how deeply complex, mysterious and difficult connection can be. Add children to the dynamic and its complexity and wonder multiply a thousand times over. Within a marriage, within a family, connection calls for attention, discipline, play, careful discernment, and much practice. As a pastor, Larry is aware that connection is at the heart of every church. It is no wonder that church units are known as congregations—places in which people congregate. He teases if he had a nickel for every church that bills itself as a "friendly church," he'd be a very rich man indeed. For many, their fundamental mission is overcoming the alienation and loneliness that characterizes modern life. Connection is the powerful and ever-changing concoction of people, things, and beliefs that matter. Humans cannot predict its impact. That lies in the province of blessing. But human beings can go out of their way to find and embrace it.

As is the case in most small rural communities, Grand Marais, Minnesota, didn't have much of a jail. There were only a few cells at the police station to hold inmates for just a short while. When Lake Superior flooded the town during a winter storm, the inmates were all recruited to help mop up the flooded town. Minnesota had a "work release" program in which inmates were released from their cells during daylight hours to perform community service. One day I asked the sheriff if the prisoners who wanted to could get out of their cells to attend church on Sunday mornings. He said he'd never been asked that before, but if we'd supply the transportation and the supervision it would be fine with him.

And so, on Sunday mornings, my wife and I took turns picking up prisoners on our way to church. One morning, the man I picked up told me that his wife had just given birth to their son. Then he shared that she had driven all the way up from Minneapolis—a four-hour drive in the best of weather—to attend church that morning. This mattered because Minnesota law prohibited him from holding his son while he was in the jail. We arrived at church. The young man walked to the first pew and sat down while a young woman holding a newborn baby entered the church and sat down near the back. The service moved along, and soon it became time for the children's message.

"Would all the children please come forward?" I asked as I did each Sunday morning. The kids loved that invitation and, as soon as the words left my mouth, a bevy of kids came forward and sat down on the low steps in front of the pulpit. To my astonishment, the prisoner also came forward and sat beside them. Then the mother came forward and gingerly gave the baby over to his father to hold and cradle for the first time. You didn't have to know anything about the young man to sense that this was a holy moment of connection that gave life to all present.

Larry

CHAPTER FOUR
Coherence

Were it not for the loss, that Monday morning held nothing special. I read the paper, listened to the news, drank a cup of coffee, completed my workout and showered to start the day. I opened the blue drawer in our kitchen that held my diabetes blood testing equipment and reached for the meter and the small bottle of test strips.

Suddenly I realized I had no idea how to make sense of the numbers. The task I had performed a thousand times before eluded me. Connie was in the living room. I went over to ask for help and began to speak with her. To my astonishment the clear sentence I had in mind came out as gibberish. I knew what I wanted to say but every attempt to speak a succinct word ended in the incoherent gibberish.

"Something's happening," I wanted to say, but out came a profusion of punctuated unintelligible sounds. Connie immediately called the hospital and we went out to the car.

She couldn't find the keys, but I saw them in the ignition and tried to tell her I had them.

"Here they are," my mind said, as more gibberish streamed forth from my lips. We arrived at the hospital. I saw friends Linda, Micki, and Doug, and Kirby, my doctor, but could not say their names or say anything to them. For the rest of the morning every clear thought, every desired expression emerged in utter and complete chaos. Nobody knew what was happening except Connie who had correctly assessed the serious nature of the situation. Some thought it was a transient ischemic attack (TIA). My doctor thought it was stress. The previous day I had told the congregation I would have to leave for a while if I was to heal from the trauma of the first stroke in November. Perhaps my words matched the incoherence I felt in my soul as I prepared to leave the friends, church and town that formed a world of meaning I loved and respected.

It turned out to be neither stress nor a TIA. An MRI showed that a second stroke had hit the language center on the left side of my brain, prompting the morning's chaos. Take away coherence and the gift of community cannot be named. The loss of coherence is an unmistakable signal that something is amiss in the fundamental health of an individual. In like manner what is true for an individual applies to a church, a community, or a nation. Coherence, and the world of meaning it invites us to share, is a leading cause of life.

Larry

—⧉—

Aaron Antonovsky believed that coherence held the key to unraveling the mystery of health.[43] Confounded by human resilience and the capacity for regeneration in the midst of the most terrible circumstances, Antonovsky followed the thread of story into the heart of human life. What distinguishes generative human life is the presence of coherence. Human life is sustained by—caused by—this coherence.

Coherence can be described as a master narrative held so deeply that it goes beneath language and into consciousness. Simply put, coherence is a sense that life makes sense, that what happens is comprehensible, that events are not random but, at least, somewhat predictable as a whole. Life is a whole that is not hostile. Even the most profoundly disruptive phenomenon—the Nazi gas chambers—is understandable

Take away coherence and the gift of community cannot be named. The loss of coherence is an unmistakable signal that something is amiss in the fundamental health of an individual. Coherence, and the world of meaning it invites us to share, is a leading cause of life.

in a way that does not leave us powerless and passive. We do not need to descend into the world of pure evil dominated only by raw power and violence. Even there, kindness and love find a way. At least they do in the lives of those who remain human.

For Beate Jakob, MD, a staff member at the German Institute for Medical Mission, coherence as a Leading Cause of Life is anything but new. After receiving her medical degree she studied Logotherapy, an approach to psychiatry developed by Viktor Frankl, a Jewish psychiatrist who was sent to Auschwitz and Dachau during WWII. During his imprisonment he noticed a difference between those who were most likely to survive and those who succumbed to the unimaginable horror of the camps.

His observation led to the founding of Logotherapy and left an indelible impact on Jakob. "Frankl later said," Jakob said, "'This was the lesson I had to learn in three years spent in Auschwitz and Dachau: those most apt to survive the camps were those oriented toward the future, toward a meaning to be fulfilled by them in the future.'" As Frankl wrote, "The meaning of our existence is not invented by ourselves, but is rather detected." One day as he witnessed yet another murder, he realized there was absolutely nothing he could do to stop the atrocity. But he could reach within himself and reframe the way he reacted to it. In that moment, and in the ensuing years, he began to develop the principles of Logotherapy.

"My training in Logotherapy was a turning point in my life," said Jakob. "I saw that my personal history is not determining my future. Instead, I can determine the possibilities myself. In psychotherapy people often say their lives are bad from the beginning, and that they have no chance of changing things. But in Logotherapy we tell people that things go wrong in everyone's life, and yet everybody has the chance to become somebody. Frankl's own life is an example. The German title of his book is *Say Yes to Life*."[44]

Responsible for theological inquiry at Difaem, Jakob realizes that finding and affirming a thread of coherence in life has spiritual implications. But she is also clear that coherence is not restricted to people of faith. "The search for meaning leads us to the point of God," she said. "But people not believing in God can also say life is meaningful. Logotherapy applies to everyone.

"In personal life," Jakob said, "people tend to look at the deficiencies and say, 'That is going wrong.' The key is to look at what is thriving. I am always trying to get this message out to the parishes. I often give small lectures in parishes about health and healing. As I do, I am always talking about strengths and available resources that are so often overlooked. In German parishes people will say, 'We don't have enough money, or enough people, or enough of this and that.' It is so important to help them look at their assets."

Through her own experience, Jakob has seen the importance of speaking the language of life in the healing process.

"I'm a medical doctor who worked at a hospital before I joined Difaem," she said. "I often saw people who received every treatment we had, but they didn't get better. Then, when the chaplain visited, they improved. There is a multidimensional unity of healing. The doctor, the sociologist, the psychologist, and the congregation are all part of a therapeutic team, and each has an essential role."

—⁂—

Humans—*Homo sapiens sapiens*—are conscious of being conscious. We know we know; we think about thinking. We know we are telling a story when we are talking to each other. We live suspended in a narrative that quite literally gives us life. Our most primal symbols represent this knowing: the Word of Life, *Logos*, the tree of knowledge before which there is no humanity, and after which humanity is possible. We cannot tolerate incoherence because coherence ties together not just thought, but all that connects us. Coherence gives our choices purpose and hope. Coherence is so vital that we rightly fear incoherence as a fundamental threat. That's why religion is so commonly linked to violence, even when what is being fought over is really much more mundane and obvious—land, money, privilege. The violence in Darfur, Lebanon, Baghdad, or Rwanda is exactly *not* about religion, although the winners and losers can be sorted out by their religious affiliations. Evangelicals turn venom toward the gay and lesbian community not because they are afraid of seduction, but because a gay lifestyle undermines the coherence of their master narrative. The story holding their life together frays at the edges and starts to unravel. Easier to fight the unraveling at its edge than to ask whether the whole fabric is out of whack.

Coherence gives our choices purpose and hope.

Human life is sustained by a coherence that generates adaptivity and manages complex relationships. There are other forms of coherence that function quite differently, each of which has its priests, myths, rituals, and stories that work for better and worse depending on the circumstances. The Reverend Dr. Martin Luther King Jr. presented a highly coherent view of life in these United States that subverted the master narrative that had so successfully held together pathological oppression, poverty, and powerlessness based on race.[45] When he rolled into Memphis, it was not surprising that he found almost all of the white religious leaders lined up ready to drip their type of Christian icing over the racist cake. These white leaders helped make oppression coherent and thus strong. But King's coherence made their story incoherent, and thus threatened its life. The bullet that killed him was just a footnote that could have come in a hundred other towns King's master story subverted.

King did not fear this fight among master stories, because he felt that the story of a loving, just, patient God was a better fit for reality than the brittle, unfair God of the time. King bet his life that the arc of history would bend toward justice. His story did not depend on his own personal longevity. We're still waiting to see how the story turns out.

Some religions serve life better than others. Some that would appear to share the vocabulary of life actually make life less likely to be sustained. King knew this in his bones, not just his head, and it flowed through his life like good water on good soil. The best religion is that which reminds us of who we are and where our life originates.

We have about 3,000 patients passing through our doors at Methodist Healthcare on any given day; about two-thirds of these patients spend just one day with us. The others are on a healing journey that includes an average of about five and a half days inside our walls. Even in the best of circumstances a hospital is inevitably a place of great fear and uncertainty. People who function quite well outside the walls find a vulnerability that presents them with a world in which things don't make much sense because they've never encountered them. My body without cancer is a whole different thing than my body with cancer. My family with everyone healthy is an entirely different world than Larry's family where chronic conditions are present in each of their lives. The coherence that held my life together could bend and may shatter under the weight of these new and unanticipated realities.

We have seven chapels in our downtown hospital. Each one has a three-ring notebook that stands on a pedestal near the entrance in which people can write their prayers. We have at least nine years of boxes filled with pages of handwritten prayers. Some of these prayers are written in the large block letters of someone who doesn't write very much. Other prayers fill the page with the small, tight script of someone journaling intensely. Most of the prayers are in blue or black ink, some in pencil. Something on the pages seems to express release—perhaps that if God would read the prayer it would improve the chance of divine intervention. The very least we can do is keep these prayers, these sacred offerings, and so we do, leaving the rest to God.

From time to time I read these prayers. They are plaintive, desperate, hopeful, manipulative, grateful, and very, very real. I wonder what happens to those whose prayers are broken under the weight of an unhealed loved one. I imagine the clear, blue joy of an answered prayer. These amazing soul mementos map connection and disconnection, hope and hopelessness, coherence and incoherence.

We have eighteen chaplains who work exactly at this dangerous juncture between incoherence and coherence. Patients who do not have a way of understanding the new world in which they find themselves are not likely to heal physically, much less find sustainable life on the other end of their journeys through our halls. A family that cannot find a new coherence after losing their mom is not likely to sustain its life as a family. Any first year nurse sees the mystery of patients coming in with identical symptoms, receiving identical treatment, and ending up with very different results. The mystery exposes one patient on an obvious journey toward life, and the other equally obviously heading toward illness and death.

> **Coherence reminds us of the web of blessing that defines our role as humans, and calls us beyond ourselves to the lives of others. Coherence gives us life.**

Sometimes persons' sense of coherence gives them the capacity to be agents in their own healing: they have a reason to take their medicine, do their exercise, and seek their own life. It may or may not be enough, but it frequently tilts the balance. Coherence gives us a way of seeing and trusting the connections across which life might flow. Those connections could be doctors and nurses, people in our congregations, schools, or neighborhoods who will hold us up until we heal, and have a chance to return the favor. Coherence reminds us of the web of blessing that defines our role as humans, and calls us beyond ourselves to the lives of others. Coherence gives us life.

—∿—

Coherence—belonging and finding meaning—is necessary for all forms of human life, including the institutions that grow from our relationships. It is helpful to see the hospital itself as being alive in this way. There are few structures that find adaptive innovation more difficult and fraught with friction. Mine has 10,000 employees and that makes it the second largest private employer in the region, an economic force in the city, and a political factor in the body politic. A hospital frequently feels utterly incoherent to those inside it, and not just to the patients disoriented by the sudden vulnerability of their illness. The environment of those working in the hospital can find their lives driven this way by that guild, that way by that payor, down a rabbit hole by that litigation, and up the other tree by a disruptive competing group with a technology nobody anticipated. But amid these confusing crosscurrents, you still find a deep current that is surprisingly coherent. If you stop almost any person or persons, from the CEO to the guy watching the parking lot, and ask them what the point is, they'll say something like: "We're here to take care of the whole community." As a public health person, I would like to encourage everyone to lean more toward prevention instead of waiting until someone has to crawl in the door. I'd prefer something like: "We're a healing presence in the whole community." But that is a relative quibble. We're here for everybody. And the reason? Oh, we're Methodist; that's the way religious folks are supposed to be.

> ## Coherence—belonging and finding meaning—is necessary for all forms of human life, including the institutions that grow from our relationships.

That's a bundle of coherence that will take you a very long way, and prevent you from making some very stupid (incoherent) kinds of choices that would violate what we recognize as life. It makes us take financial risks that others, driven by a different master narrative, would avoid. It keeps us in some neighborhoods that others leave behind. It drives us toward innovations others would find inconvenient. It enables us to look out for each other in ways that others would find needlessly complicated. That simple coherence has worked for just about nine decades, and probably will for another dozen or so. It makes us fit. It makes us connected in a way that fits the life of the community. It causes our life. That's what coherence does for any group of humans that finds a life together.

It is tempting to load more and heavier meaning onto the category of coherence, so that it comes to mean all that is ponderous and profound. Life is funny, too. People who are alive tend to notice life's irony: unexpected reversals, surprising juxtapositions of fact and fancy, wisdom in the mundane. This is funny! People who are alive notice their own mistakes of perception and sometimes find them amusing, not just tragic. Humor marks an accurate self-perception and an awareness that the cosmos does not spin on the axis of our brief handful of years. It is hard to imagine innovation coming from a lab (or a church) where laughter is not common. It is hard to imagine adaptivity in a life with no humor.

Some would see music, like humor, as an extraneous distraction to the hard slog through life. But every sustained human culture we've ever come across made music. It seems to hold us together; to carry more information, meaning, and energy than words can do by themselves (certainly more than any words can do on paper!). As I write this I am listening to the Warsaw Village Band, which a friend persuaded me to go hear when they were in Memphis. The group of young "roots" musicians has shot like a rocket out of the deep well of traditional Polish music with energy and rhythm that seems to defy gravity *and* history. I have no idea what the heck they are singing about in Polish, but I can feel the whole culture adapting right in front of my ears—especially when they dedicated the last song to Elvis.

I've listened to the sound of my own culture lurching into a new arc, too. I think back to when hundreds of Interfaith Health Program friends gathered at Ebenezer Baptist Church. This is where the Kings brought their best to the pulpit. We did, too: an Imam, a Rabbi, a Tibetan Buddhist, and another great black preacher of our own. Standing in the pulpit where King stood, all four reflected on how their faith understood King's central idea of the "beloved community." How can we, in our different ways, imagine our cities and villages as being loved by God, and thus, perhaps by us, too? How could the night end other than in singing "We Shall Overcome" in a four-part, four-faith harmony? I'm not sure I could remember exactly what any of them said, but I can remember what happened, and how it held us together, *and how alive I felt*.

—∞—

Meetings that generate life are rare. Most Thursday mornings, one or another of our staff at Methodist meets with a small group of pastors from across our region to talk about their lives and how they might be lived better. This goes back about 20 years, when it began to be apparent that clergy show remarkably unhealthy life patterns, including 20 percent greater incidence of obesity, than people their same age and a depressing amount of stress-related diseases.[46] We give the clergy an "executive physical" that frequently turns up unanticipated problems. We also spend time with them reviewing their behavioral health risks, few of which are unanticipated. Then we talk about leading a life based on the Leading Causes of Life survey we are developing. (An online assessment is available at www.leadingcausesoflife.org.) Not surprisingly, it takes about an hour for these pastors to get over talking about their congregations and start talking about themselves. At some point we usually notice that the two Leading Causes of Life most likely to be low are coherence and agency.

Coherence? How could they be low on coherence? On a sense of belonging or meaning in their lives? These people give two or three sermons every week of their lives and help people find their own coherence every day! *And that is just the problem.* Many of the clergy feel trapped in the expectations others have for them. They feel like marketing agents for a particular brand of coherence that is inflexible and too predictable. About the last thing many people want from their pastor is theological creativity or scriptural innovation. As Antonovsky noted, coherence is powerful precisely because it makes the world somewhat predictable, so we don't want our particular pastor to be unpredictable.[47] Even if we doubt and wander, we don't want our pastor to go wandering around the theological neighborhood.

In highly stable communities a pastor may be able to live a life without ever chafing at the bit, content to munch on the theological grass inside the fence. But stable communities are few today, with none to be found within hours of our hospital. Even, maybe especially, our rural areas are blown this way and that by fundamental shifts in agricultural technology and global trade policy. The church and its marketing icon (the pastor) are the last bastions of certainty left. But, as we noted previously, the qualities of sustained human life are social "generativity," adaptivity, and complexity. To be trapped as the last bastion of the past age is simply not healthy. Even as the community changes, a pastor does not feel free to allow himself or herself to change unless he or she can find a new coherence that fits the reality of the larger world. Some hope to stick with their story at least until the retirement plan kicks in and they go find a better one in private. Others internalize the stresses, which show up as constant lower back pain, pathological eating, and long lonely hours on the job. Others find their way to another religious tribe, a tribe that allows for a different story that looks more like their kind of life. You can almost hear Antonovsky reminding us: "Hey! The miracle is how many of these pastors live lives of service, meaning, blessing, and hope for decades! How do you explain *that*?" It is certainly not because the medical world has done well, and the denominational structures even less so. It is better to explore the causes of life and to look for their expression and development as the way thriving people have learned to adapt to the changing circumstances along the way. For most clergy, when coherence is abundant and clear, it is the most consistently inspiring and generative cause of life. This may come from clergy's frequent experience of being "called" into the service of the loving, life-giving God who sustains all creation.

It was just another Sunday morning. Four people, a fifth of the congregation, gathered as they do each week before worship for a time of study and reflection. The news on that Sunday morning was of unmitigated chaos. The conflict between Israel and Hezbollah had taken a staggering toll; future conflicts waited in the wings. A plot to blow up ten jetliners had been uncovered; bombs in Baghdad continued to explode. Incoherence ran rampant. During their discussion, which couldn't help but mix the morning's headlines with Scripture, they measured a sense of faith-centered assurance against a sense of helplessness. Their vocations—selling roofs, repairing motorcycles, crafting lanterns, and overseeing the kitchen in the town's grocery store—seemed utterly disconnected from the world's greatest needs.

When the time for worship arrived, signaled by a simple prelude that settled into familiar tunes of a few well-known hymns, we all knew what the service would be about. It would be about life. It would devote itself to the affirmation of coherence in a seemingly incoherent world. Rural ministry inevitably calls us to do so. It dismisses the voices of comparison that say, "You're too small," or "You're too old," or "You're too far away from the seats of power to have any influence." And it knows that worship, and its attendant coffee hours and Bible studies, are essentially rehearsals in how to live when the rain doesn't fall, when the news takes our breath away, when illness comes our way.

A man who had just found out from an MRI that he didn't have a brain tumor despite his seizures, came forward and lit one of the candles on the altar. In the bulletin his quiet lighting of the candle was named "The Bringing of God's Light." It might just as well have been called "The Return of Hope." His simple act brought the light into darkness and in effect said, "I'm home again."

The call to worship asked, "Why are we here?" We are here to remember the promises of God. We are here to encourage each other in the living of life. We are here to rehearse what it means to be a human being who walks the line between fear and confidence with assurance. When the service moved to "A Time for Prayer," coherence once again made its presence known as the congregation lovingly named those who just received a tough diagnosis or those who were ensnared by one circumstance or another. The prayers asked for guidance, assurance, an end to violent chaos, and the blessing of community.

In different ways, the worship in a synagogue, a mosque, a temple, or a church is inevitably an exercise in the establishment of coherence. So, of course, are the board meetings of a hospital or a corporation, the forming of a choir, the running of an election, the holidays of a nation, the celebrating of an anniversary or a birthday. One could say it is all about coherence. But that's not actually true. It would be better to say that it is about practiced coherence. Left on its own, coherence can run amok. Although it can encourage benevolence, it can also fan the fires of cruelty. The coherence that has the power to say, "This is who we are" quickly, and sometimes violently, adds, "And this is who you are not." The drive for coherence is powerful enough to form gangs, powerful enough to cook the books of a corporation in an attempt to show that all is well, powerful enough to red line urban districts, leave fruit rotting in the orchards because of concern over the status of those who pick peaches, clean the office buildings, and engage in so many other endeavors. In most American cities there is not one council of churches or ministerial alliance, there are two or three because the "saved" shun fellowship with the "less faithful." Reformed, orthodox, mainline, evangelical, Shiite, Sunni, and liturgy itself—all reflect a search for coherence.

It did not surprise me when I noticed that each of our causes had a corresponding liturgy in the church year. In the Christian year Advent is all about connection as the Word is made flesh and the angels sing in the night sky. Lent, to my ears, is about coherence as we center our lives on the holy and try to trim the distractions that take us away from both God and neighbor. Easter is about hope. And Pentecost centers on agency as the church receives the empowering Spirit. The many months between Pentecost and Advent are days of blessing as "ordinary time" proves to be anything but ordinary in light of the preceding seasons. In short, the liturgical seasons also provide coherence and shed new light on life.

Why do we seek coherence? It is tied to the very way we perceive life. For every thought a person has there are thousands, even millions, of other thoughts that do not take root in action or a world of meaning. There are so many things happening at any given point in time that the brain needs—and thankfully has—many filters to determine which perceptions are necessary to establish the order. Damage those filters and life suddenly becomes overwhelming. With the filters in place, buying groceries at the corner store or in a supermarket is a simple task to navigate. One tunes out the beeps of a scanner machine, the sounds of conversation, the movements of people as they make their way through the line. But if you damage those filters, each one of those sights and sounds claims center stage, resulting in chaos, anxiety, and often chronic fatigue. It is exhausting to live without coherence. In other words, we are neurologically wired to establish coherence.

—∿—

Voice is yet another way to frame the power of coherence. What does it mean when we say a writer has found his or her voice? Likewise, what does it mean when we say a person has missed his or her calling? In the first case, authenticity has been found. In the second case, incoherence prevails. We believe that the search for voice calls us to life. We also believe this is easier said than done.

Within the life of many churches, the word "confirmation" (when a 13- or 14-year-old lays claim to his or her faith as an adult) is an anticipated but often dreaded word. Kids and their parents often resolve to get "through it." Confirmands (those preparing for confirmation) are frequently expected to memorize the books of the Bible, to take sermon notes or recite knowledge the pastor or priest wants them to know. In short, they are to give voice to their faith in a voice that is anything but their own. But it doesn't have to be that way if we will just respect and look for an authentic voice.

Jared was not a member of my church. I met him while working with his family as a hospice chaplain. His father was slowly and inexorably succumbing to cancer. After his father died, Jared asked if he could become part of the confirmation program in my church. He knew what this would entail. The yearlong assignment for the confirmands was simple: on a given Sunday each would stand before the congregation and speak the truth about their own lives and God. Each one would choose the hymns, offer the prayers, decorate the church, and give the sermon based on one of twelve Bible stories he or she studied throughout the year.

To my surprise, the story Jared chose to frame his life was the story of Jesus healing the boy possessed by demons. It was intriguing that Jared chose a healing story when prayers for his father had fallen short. But the reason for his choice became clear as Jared stood in the pulpit and began to give his sermon.

"The story of the possessed relates to me in a lot of ways. Why could Jesus take the evil spirit right out of a little boy, but didn't take the evil spirit of cancer out of my dad? My dad had some hip problems and some handicaps that made him unable to do a lot of stuff with me that he would have liked to do. Then he got cancer. I thought that God would give him a break and heal him. But for some reason God did not help my dad. My dad still had lots of time to live, time to take me fishing, and teach me many a thing. Now I have to live with watching my friends with their dads, and listen to them talk about what they did over the weekend with their dads. I really want to say what I did over the weekend with my dad, but I can't.

"But that hasn't been the hardest thing yet. I had to watch my dad die. I came home from school knowing that my dad was going to die. I used to come home, go into my room, and just cry because I knew that in a couple of months I would not be able to do anything with my dad anymore.

"After my dad died I started to miss my grandpa even more, because he died when I was real little. I have always wanted to learn to fly fish, and I was hoping my grandpa would be able to teach me. But luckily he taught my uncles how to fly fish really well, so now, when I go fishing with one of them, they always say that grandpa says to do it this way.

"I am just glad that God is still with us, and keeps us together. Sometimes I wonder if God is looking out after us when things aren't going well. I like to think he is, but he sure didn't seem to be here when my dad was dying. I felt like God forgot about us, or didn't see us. I believed he would help until the day my dad died, then I lost hope for the longest time. Then I began to think about what else there was in life.

"And then I finally started to have faith in God again. Like the possessed boy, I was possessed by sadness. But now, it is healing. That is why I chose this story. I chose it because it relates to me in many ways. And now that I have written this paper, I see how much more it relates to me than before."

By now the entire congregation, which had learned to keep a box of tissues beneath each of the pews, was in tears. They saw this young man find a voice that linked a biblical story with the events of his life. They were proud of him, awed by him emotionally, and spiritually moved by him. In short, he found his voice that brought together and transcended the events of his life. He had found and shared life's gift of coherence.

Never say it's just a story. If you want to look for life, the stories that serve life might be just the place to begin.

Larry

CHAPTER FIVE
Agency

" There are times the power of agency becomes stunningly clear,"
writes Larry. "We had nothing," she said. The small village of
Makhoba had been part of the Transkie, one of the desolate "home-
lands" created by the apartheid South African government for
blacks. For years the primary purpose of the village was to supply
workers for the mines or industry in Johannesburg or elsewhere. It
existed to serve the needs of another culture. The disparity between
the beautiful, productive fields of the white-owned farms a few
miles away and the plight of this village was overwhelming. But the
speaker, and the 30 or so people who surrounded her in the small
house as the rain fell, soon began to tell the story of the Phakamani
Project they had been sharing with Bob Thelin, an agronomist missionary who spent the better part of his life in Africa. *Phakamani*
means to "get up." The story couldn't help but be one of agency.

"We thought we had nothing," the woman said. "But then we
began to realize we had everything we needed. In the beginning of

the Bible it says that God created the world and it was good. God brought forth vegetation, and it was good. For so long we had been thinking that anything good was far away. We had been thinking that 'distant' Johannesburg is life. We had been thinking that our sons and daughters had to get away from here. We had been thinking we had nothing. But that is not true. God gave us everything we need if we would just open our eyes. God gave us seeds. God gives us rain. God gives us ways to replenish the soil."

They had seen the revival of a neighboring village whose people organized to build cisterns that gathered rainwater they then used to irrigate a well-mulched garden that provided a source of income, how proceeds from a bakery funded a small nursery, how homemade candles put money in the treasury, how a fencing project prevented over-grazing. They saw all this and wanted to reclaim their land and their lives as well.

Humans do. We go here or there, now or later, fast or slow. We do, lift, reach, touch, hold, dig, study, watch, fight, love, seek, wait, and stand. We do, and thus we live. Sometimes all we have is this doing. Sometimes doing may be enough to keep us alive until the other Leading Causes of Life rise into the space created by our doing. Doing is a kind of thinking, for it embeds and expresses choice among options.

Sometimes doing is a high order of thinking. When the Civil Rights movement hung by a slender thread, its young leaders were baffled by storms of violence and political cynicism beyond what they had anticipated in their darkest imaginations. They argued strategy through the night—whether to go back to the violent streets, into the courts, back to the churches, around the schools, or to withdraw until they could figure it all out. John Lewis, all of 23 years old, said, "I'm marching." They argued for another hour until Lewis said again, "I'm marching." Again they debated, wearing themselves out in analysis. The next morning, Lewis got up and marched.[48] So did hundreds of others. It was all they could do at that moment, and so they did. Lewis was an agent in his own life; he expressed agency. He moved, chose, acted. That expression of agency created hope when there was none to be found. It will be remembered as a blessing long after Lewis lays his body down. It connected people who had been shattered. It created the possibility of coherence where there was little left.

As Larry finished his work on this book, a fire south of his town in Montana had already claimed over 100,000 acres, and afternoon winds were expected to reach 40 miles an hour. The fire camp stationed hundreds of fire fighters, the hotshots were expected to arrive, and a family had to be rescued by helicopter. The basement of the United Church of Christ he served was given over to the Forest Service, state officials, local fire officials, civil defense folks—a maze of people all coordinating their various agencies, all acting, all doing something in response to a fire whose energy could not be contained. It was a stunning example of agency and agencies in action. One does not need to look far to find similar examples of agency: the ER room of a hospital, Meals-on-Wheels meal delivery, or even the wheels of war. But there is another side to agency when we apply it to the Leading Causes of Life.

—⁓—

Agency is a generative force that inevitably leads to the matter of call. It gives traction to three questions: "What am I to do with my life?" "What have I been called to do?" and "Am I doing it?"

Several years ago, the Alban Institute, an organization devoted to studying and helping congregations, conducted a study analyzing the "state of the church" in the United States. It noted that fewer and fewer individuals were choosing ministry as a lifelong calling. It found that the perception of church as a place of creative and meaningful endeavor was eroding.[49] It is not surprising that clergy so often rank themselves as low when it comes to agency and coherence. Indeed, when many clergy leave a parish they decide to leave ministry entirely. In an effort to help, the Louisville Institute, funded by the Lilly Foundation, created a fund to provide sabbatical time for clergy whose churches could not afford to fund that.[50] The Louisville Institute then went out of its way to gather those receiving a fellowship before they headed out on their sabbatical journey, including Larry. Their orientation was built around a single word: *agency*.

Larry remembers the word surprising him. He rarely heard it used outside of an institutional reference point.

"The time you are about to take is all about recovering the gift of agency," the speaker said to Larry and his colleagues.

"It's all about *agency*," the speaker said again, carefully, letting the word ring for a moment. And then he began to unpack its meaning. Were Larry to paraphrase the speaker's ensuing comments it would go something like this:

> Just as *hope* is different from wishful thinking, and *blessing* is more than a nice thing to say, so *agency* has the capacity to transcend mere activity. Agency is an action, but it is also a gift when aligned with purpose or call.

"There are so many concerns in your lives, so many conflicts, so many things to think about that it is almost easy to forget your true calling. It is easy to put your creative powers, and your relationship with the call that brought you to ministry, on the back burner. But in these coming months you have time to uncover those embers. It is important that you take time away from your community. It is important that you not see this time as 'work.' Yes, you may write a book. Or, yes, you may accomplish the plan you submitted. But the most important thing is to recover the gift of agency that sometimes almost fades away in all of us. Your sabbatical is a time to recover your call and to renew your engagement in mission. It is about agency.

"Just as *hope* is different from wishful thinking, and *blessing* is more than a nice thing to say, so *agency* has the capacity to transcend mere activity. Agency is an action, but it is also a gift when aligned with purpose or call. I think of physicians who freely give of their time to see patients without worrying about how many minutes a visit lasts or what the payment code should be. Why do so many relish the thought of lending their healing skills to the people of Haiti or Paraguay or Mexico or mission stations throughout the United States? They do so to recover their call—to nourish the power of agency in their lives."

It is agency that turns abstract nouns into verbs. Agency turns connection into connect, build, reach, touch, embrace, and heal. It transforms the aura of hope into leadership fearless enough to find light at the end of discouraging labyrinths. It is agency that moves coherence into the realm of decision, which defines the boundaries of any community, project, or endeavor. It is agency that insists blessing lead to a new perception. And it is agency that harnesses the perception of call.

The name of God as given in Hebrew Scripture, I AM WHAT I AM, is a verb, not a noun. It could as well be translated, I DO WHAT I DO. Indeed it is impossible to say "God" without saying "Agency."

—∞—

Agency is the human capacity to do. Steve DeGruchy, one of our colleagues in the Africa Religious Health Assets Program, brought agency into the heart of our research on assets.[51] Steve has students from all across Africa who come to study the link between theology and the development of their communities, which are almost all held in the grip of poverty. They find his focus on "assets" electrifying as it turns the passive victims of poverty into active agents capable of acting to break the cycle of oppression that seems to mock God's promise of life. Speaking of the poor, Steve writes that, "they cannot be passengers on the journey, but find their own sense of freedom via their agency in the struggle for freedom. And because this is dialogical action, this agency is not

> It is agency that turns abstract nouns into verbs. Agency turns connection into connect, build, reach, touch, embrace, and heal. It transforms the aura of hope into leadership fearless enough to find light at the end of discouraging labyrinths.

simply expressed through action in some sort of politburo-led, revolutionary cannon-fodder way, but also through reflection. It is crucial that the insights, perspectives, rituals, and symbols of the poor contribute to the very vision of the future that is being sought. Action and theory thus find expression in liberating praxis."[52]

We do because we reflect; we reflect because we are capable of doing.

As the swell of AIDS orphans reached tidal proportions, UNICEF and others wondered what kind and scale of response was possible. The obvious one—orphanages—was impossible. How could we build and sustain orphanages for 20 million children amid already broken African economies? They launched a small study in just six countries to evaluate what might be done by the world's humanitarian agencies.[53] To everyone's surprise, they learned that small groups of village women had already moved quietly, but on a very large scale. On average, each group of women (usually members of a small church) was taking care of about a hundred kids, sort of like a perpetual, full-service summer camp. This was happening in thousands of villages without any encouragement, training, or funding from the big agencies from afar that were thought to be indispensable in such work.

Agency is the human capacity to do.

These women expressed their own agency, not waiting or even thinking about waiting for any agencies. They simply did what they could do. While, in most villages, the male preachers were still going on about AIDS being a punishment from God—and perpetuating the worst stigmas imaginable about these kids—the women simply did what they knew to do. Most of them could not possibly explain the etiology of the HIV virus or how it spreads. But they fed and sheltered the kids and found ways to clothe and protect them as was possible. They had nowhere to march, so they stayed put, caring for the dying mothers, and welcoming back the older kids coming home to die. At the same time, they gave the young ones a chance at life. Many of those kids will end up fine, although many will not.

Such agency creates the possibility of more agency. We've seen this in the development of the women's project called Masangane, which means, "We embrace."[54] Masangane exists in the rural Eastern

Cape of South Africa, although it could be in a thousand other African provinces. A women's project linked to the local churches, Masangane began as an orphans program. As anti-retroviral therapy (ART) dropped in price, Masangane began to morph into an ART delivery program. In most of Africa, ART is still quite difficult to manage and administer once you get out of walking distance of the urban research hospitals. But the history of doing by these women laid a strong foundation of confidence and trust on which ARTs could find their way into the lives of the women who needed them. Where the government clinics take months to qualify a person and begin treatment, Masangane gets someone on the medicine in days.[55] And they take care of the kids in the meantime. Agency creates more agency, and it generates the space for the other causes of life along the way. The social network that comes into being in this process is complex, weaving in experts of several nations, multiple faiths, and diverse backgrounds. The community adapts; it lives.

The Masangane women's agency makes life more coherent to those left behind—it models the agency that the daughters and sons will need as they grow up much too fast into a very hostile world. It gives hope where none would be expected. It gives life.

You could argue it the other way around—beginning the story with the connections among the women, stressing their shared sense of meaning supported by the church, their

Agency creates more agency, and it generates the space for the other causes of life along the way.

powerful identity as agents of blessing and tending across the generations. Who cares which way the causes spin, or which cause generates the other? As the women show, where you have one, you'll find the others. Life comes from life, and soon spins into the full ensemble. The point is, if you ever find yourself in an African village wondering how it will adapt to the incredible challenges it so obviously faces, go look for a group of women and some kids. Watch what they do.

—⁓—

In his book *Careless Society*, John McKnight documents how professional helpers can undermine the agency of communities.[56] This observation is always a deep offense to seminary and public health students who are paying a lot of money to prepare for relatively low-paying careers helping people. Of course, people like John and me get paid by universities to prepare students to enter into these careers. John's uncomfortable point is that we must be careful that the expression of our organizations doesn't suppress the agency of the people we are supposed to be helping. UNICEF works hard to avoid making this deadly mistake, as do the best of clergy, and the most successful of physicians and community organizers. It takes both courage and art to foster the agency of those who could be taught to be grateful for their crippling dependency. Clergy undermine the life of their congregations when they do all the theological work for their members, suppressing the natural curiosity necessary for mature faith. Doctors do that when they give prescriptions instead of education about the process of health. The iron rule of community organizing is to never do for any one what the individuals or groups can do for themselves. This is because agency is a sacred, generative well of life to be tended with reverence.

> **It seems that the whole human body is designed to grow on its own capacity to do, which, if unexercised, atrophies.**

The wise nurse on the cancer ward nurtures the agency of the patients, finding ways for them to express choice, even if it is just between cereal or oatmeal for breakfast. A physical therapist pulls the patients onto their feet and down the hall after a shockingly brief period of passive rest. It seems that the whole human body is designed to grow on its own capacity to do, which, if unexercised, atrophies. Orthopedic patients would rarely believe they could stand, much less walk, so soon. The only way they learn is to do. If this is true for muscles and bone, how much more true is it for the spirit, the mind, and hope, itself?

Kindness can disable, crossing the line into a self-serving business plan. John McKnight painfully counts the cash that flows into a community in the name of health, finding that nearly all of it stops in the pockets of the professionals providing formal services for the people.[57] The cycle is self-reinforcing because it has a kind of pathological coherence. Soon people forget their own capacities, doubting the value of anything not provided by someone in a uniform with letters behind their name.

The single most humane place in the entire modern health system is hospice, where, as you approach your very last days, you can reasonably expect to have all the religious professionals, scientific experts, volunteers, even the insurance companies aligned with each other around your humanity. A friend has pointed out that one shouldn't have to die to experience that, but for the most part, you do. Even here, where the systems have grown in sophisticated compassion, their very competence can be disabling to the informal networks of care that grow organically among neighbors and members of faith communities. The care once provided quite well by a living community can be replaced by—not augmented by—a service underwritten by somebody else. Deprived of agency, even at its most intimate moments, a family dies. So, too, a community. Agency devolves into passivity, which feeds dependence contingent on others' whimsical or rented good intentions. The breath goes out; fear comes in.

Agency does the opposite. Lewis marched. The African mothers tended the kids. A good hospice nurtures the life of the family even as the loved one passes on. They generated a little space into which crept hope. So they marched and cared again. We think that very large-scale problems demand very large, well thought out answers: AIDS, global warming, pollution of the Mississippi river, intractable racism. Surely we cannot begin until we have thought it all through, until we have a clear course of action that will solve the problem. So we wait. In Memphis, the spiral of tangled problems has created a knot so complex that a healthy and successful generation of kids is almost beyond imagination. Those who know the most about the problem are the ones most locked in place. My role at the health system makes me an easy target for an endless stream of confounding discussions about these problems. Early childhood is a recurrent conversation, at least once a month on average. We go down the rabbit holes of unwed mothers, poor nutrition, underweight babies, bad education, terrible housing, and the understimulation of the kids that leads to under-developed brains. Then we predictably loop through the failure of political, community, and religious leaders to fully appreciate the debacle. We usually end up with some scheme to gather them all into a mega-summit in which we can finally, once and for all, name the monster that is killing our kids and our future. But as Steve DeGruchy points out, nobody ever built a community out of what it didn't have. We can't do what we don't do. We need to discover our agency to crack the negative monolith. A map of what is already emerging in the life our kids would, as it did in Africa, probably consist of a surprising swarm of efforts moving up among those we think are unqualified to make big decisions. A map of the assets relevant to our fears would show us agency where we least expect it, and at a scale that would confront us with inconvenient hope. Agency does. In the process, it cracks open space for more fully developed life to thrive.

—ⱳ—

Jody Kretzmann directs the Institute for Policy Research at Northwestern University. He is clear about how important agency is—and equally clear about how often it is missed. In the late 1960's, he developed a program in community organizing for the Associated Colleges of the Midwest, designed to help students overcome the injustices and inequalities that were, and are, so much a part of the system. He first used the principles of Saul Alinsky that involved organizing around particular issues in order to solve them.

"I ended up thinking that issue-related organizing is very important, but in it you are trying to put together a powerful neighborhood base in order to assess mostly outside forces," he said in an interview with Larry. "For example, you might get a group to go after landlords who don't live in the community, or to attack a city police that was clearly harmful. It is designed to hold institutions accountable. That is well and good, but it sometimes reinforces the deficiency idea, the idea that the community can't find solutions to the problems it is facing.

"We began to think, 'That's half of what needs to be done.' The other half is bringing people together to recognize their capacity to do problem solving themselves. This is different from banding together against outside forces and trying to change them. That points to the agency concept in your Leading Causes of Life. When people think that other people are the solution all the time, or that somebody else has the answer, they lose the capacity to be an agent.

112

"Creative neighborhood leaders . . . are discovering that wherever there are effective community development efforts, those efforts are based upon an understanding, or a map, of the community's assets, capacities, and abilities. It is clear that even the poorest neighborhood is a place where individuals and organizations represent resources upon which to rebuild. The key to neighborhood regeneration, then, is to locate all of the available local assets, to connect them with one another in ways that multiply their power and effectiveness."

The resulting map will not focus solely on how many arrests there have been, how many fires, how many residents receive food stamps, how many drop out of high school, how many are turned away from overcrowded emergency rooms, how many lack afterschool programs, or how many live in fear. Instead the map and the mappers take pains to find signs of life.

"We have to encourage people to be listeners," said Jody. "At a place like Northwestern University where there are lots of wonderful young people who have no experience in inner city communities, we teach them that, when you enter a place, you lead with your ears and not with your mouth.

"Every community has five assets. The first is simply the people who live there. It is important to push away the labels of 'needy' or 'deficient.' In other words, one keeps away from saying, 'pregnant teen' and listens instead to a young person with a voice. We find that there are hundreds and hundreds of people walking with each other in the life of any community.

"The second category of assets is face-to-face voluntary associations, such as church groups or service organizations. The third category is institutional in nature. It involves the places where paid people do the work—the schools, libraries, and parks, for example. The fourth involves the physical assets of the community and the fifth is about economic activity. We think successful community development connects those five things, and mobilizes them around a vision for the future. It is all about how one does *life* as opposed to how you solve a particular problem.

"One consistent conceptual theme in our work is that people get marginalized when they are regarded primarily as problems. They may be seen as too old, or too young, or too disabled. Once they are

113

labeled as problems nobody ever asks them for their gifts. Nobody even opens up the possibility that they can contribute. So the lack of agency, to use the Leading Causes of Life language, is one way of understanding how marginalization happens."

Detecting the presence of agency is at the heart of Jody's approach. If the problems and injustices that pervade the human landscape are to be healed, the language of life must be spoken.

"In response to the desperate situation [of many communities], well-intended people seek solutions by taking one of two divergent paths. The first, which begins by focusing on a community's needs, deficits and problems, is still by far the most traveled, and commands the vast majority of our financial and human resources. By comparison with the second path, which insists on beginning with a clear commitment to discovering a community's capacities and assets, and which is the direction [we] recommend, the first and more traditional path is more like an eight-lane superhighway."

For Jody, the son of a minister, it is not surprising that there are spiritual underpinnings to his work.

"I frequently refer to the passage in John where, just before Jesus dies, he tells his disciples that he doesn't want them to be servants anymore—they are to be friends. That is a really important transition. A good community is made up of friends, not people who get services delivered to them."

—m—

I've always been attracted to the mountain cliffs of North Georgia, not because I love rocks, but because among the rocks you can always find pine trees growing right out into the wind. They simply do not know enough to quit, and so they don't. They live. The seed grows where it has been blown, puts down a laughably slender root into too-shallow dust, and starts to suck in the light and water. Over the next winter, the roots channel water a bit further into the cracked rock. The water freezes, making way for the root to push further the next spring. I like that. That's agency.

Agency is more likely to grunt than sing, more likely to burst into sweat than into rhyme. Sometimes it picks up and moves. Greg Fricchione points out that humans have always moved toward and away from things. We are living amid one of the largest scale human movements our species has ever experienced. Millions move across porous national boundaries, driven by wars and environmental destruction. Some are drawn to the economic magnets millions know as Cape Town and Los Angeles, while others find themselves moving toward small Western Kansas towns or tiny islands of Indonesia guided only by the word of family members. People do by moving. Sometimes it is all they can do. As they move, they often find themselves adapting to complex new environments in which their old reflexes, vocabulary, and skills are out of context, maybe entirely irrelevant. And sometimes not.

Jim Cochrane, my friend and a teacher at the University of Cape Town, lives about 100 yards from what has become in the past several years a settlement of 25,000 people who moved from all over southern Africa. This is happening all over the developing world, but this particular little settlement is just up the hill from him. The town, predictably named after Nelson Mandela, was at first just a miasma of shanties. It seemed entirely without resources, a pure burden on the government down the hill. Jim's wife, Renata, noticed the emergence of a thin fiber of trust visible in a house church convened by one of the immigrants who happened to be an Angolan minister. That social hub was just barely stable enough for it to be noticed by local churches

This is how the Leading Causes of Life function—not as a sequence, but as a tightly bound ensemble, one causing the other in a tumbling emergent process that generates and adapts to a complex social web that manages to sustain itself.

that worked with the city to get a fresh water pipe up the hill. Several years later, a much thicker web of connections has formed around that little house church, which now has its own branch of Habitat for Humanity. As I've gone back to see Jim and Renata year after year, I've noticed that down near the bottom of the hill the Habitat houses are starting to be the norm, instead of the shacks. There's something that looks like a store (sort of like

Roxie's in Uptown Memphis), and other churches are finding their way too. It has started to look like a neighborhood with a life.

The point is that when persons express their agency by moving a thousand miles into a very strange land, they do not strip off all their former life in the process. Some of that life, such as those beliefs that give coherence and hope, grow as seeds in the new land that agency has found. Their new life comes from their old life. This new life is not the same, but not entirely new, either. This is how the Leading Causes of Life function—not as a sequence, but as a tightly bound ensemble, one causing the other in a tumbling emergent process that generates and adapts to a complex social web that manages to sustain itself.

—✳—

Sometimes when groups of persons express agency over time, they end up creating agencies. The hospital I work for is one such expression, a crystallization of decades of agency. It is common for agencies such as ours to be a bit dim about how very much agency we have that is relevant beyond our narrowly focused identity as a hospital. We do medicine, we think. Actually, we do life, which includes pretty large-scale public projects and urban redevelopment. We are currently building hundreds of millions of dollars of construction—everything from a children's hospital to a hospice, adult emergency rooms to an urban retreat center. We spark the construction of homes and laboratories, and create a vortex that draws in all sorts of other office buildings and, being Memphis, several barbecue restaurants. Some of this agency is expressed on purpose, but much is not. We're getting more and more focused on the full picture. Our Board of Directors approved, for the first time, a corporate strategy that specifically calls for building a web of community partnerships. That will mean expressing the agency necessary for creating a large number of complex social relationships that we will not, and cannot, own like buildings. This kind of agency is a team sport with goals and processes that only emerge in the midst of the relationship. This kind of doing is a kind of thinking that is only partly purposeful. We don't know exactly what is possible until we move into partnerships that find their own life, their own agency, and their own coherence.

About this point you should begin to sense how differently life's causes work, and the different curiosities they should evoke. If you are looking for life, don't just look for the one cause. It is important to broaden your curiosity to include any one of them. It is rare to find one cause by itself. This makes things easier, not more complicated. If you want to see agency relevant to AIDS orphans, look for the connections found among village mothers and those they love. If you want to see connection, find the places where some sort of enduring meaning is held up and nurtured. As soon as you add the qualifier "sustained" to the search (sustained connection, sustained agency) the more likely you will find all five Leading Causes of Life working as an ensemble. That's what thrives.

CHAPTER SIX
Blessing

Of all the Leading Causes of Life, blessing is perhaps the most dependent on its companions of hope, agency, coherence, and connection. A blessing that doesn't lead to hope isn't a blessing at all—it is a curse. There is no such thing as a blessing that doesn't lead to change or renewed affirmation. It is in the very nature of blessing to announce a worldview. Without connection blessings cannot happen. One cannot bless oneself. Blessings are received from others or given to others. There are few words that become such a repeated part of a pastor's vocabulary as "blessing." Larry notes that when he parts company from virtually anyone, whether it's after a "what's up" conversation on the sidewalk, talking with someone at the grocery store, or signing off on the telephone, he'll say, "God bless." The "Blessing Song" graces the end of each worship service. At potluck suppers we ask the blessing. Notice the verb: we *ask* the blessing. We *ask* for it because we cannot bestow it on or for ourselves.

Larry recalls, "I will never forget the Sunday in Big Timber, Montana, that we decided to bless the healers in our town. We sent out letters to the doctors, the nurses, the nursing home staff, the hospice team, and others whose job or title might indicate they were healers. As it invariably does, word about the service traveled throughout the church and community. We expected a dozen or so "healers" to show up to receive a blessing. But when the time came, there were far more than a dozen in line, waiting. The school nurse was there; the ombudsman at the nursing home stood in line, some of the EMTs were in line. Some belonged to our church, and others didn't. More than we had anticipated, we were a community of healers. I later realized that we hadn't just given a blessing, we had organized an entire service around it."

There is no such thing as a blessing that doesn't lead to change or renewed affirmation. It is in the very nature of blessing to announce a worldview.

Any one of us humans lives for only a brief handful of years at best. You would think we would notice, and build our theories around such an inescapable fact. But we tend to miss it. Our short longevity becomes really clear when we think of our lives in the context of truly significant natural phenomena. Henry Turley's beloved Harbor Town sits on Mud Island, which is located at the southern end of the New Madrid fault line. Most geologists think the New Madrid is overdue for another thundering earthquake of the sort that set bells ringing in Boston in 1811–1812. *This* is the disaster we worry about in Memphis, not a hurricane. This Big One will probably drop at least three of our four bridges into the Mississippi, collapse a large fraction of our schools, and pretty well wreck the day for hospital administrators. Experts say Mud Island will "liquefy," turning homes into boats. But measured against geological time, the odds of an earthquake of this magnitude happening in the years relevant to *me* (the next 30, say the life insurance experts) are not too high. I could probably buy a house there and be fine. Until I'm not.

The point is, human life is really short, so "success" cannot be measured in only one of our measly life spans. Human life has to be a social life spanning multiple generations, or it doesn't work. Each generation must adapt, using all that we have learned from those who came before us, so that all those who come after us will live, or it is not a successful strategy. That fundamental requirement is no less true now that our average life span in the U.S. has nearly doubled since my mom was born a hundred years ago (from 45 to around 82).[58] The advance, certainly the most dramatic since cave painting passed the time, was due mostly to those things we do together: inspect food, clean water, take out the trash, immunize kids, and pay enough so that we have decent housing and schools. We have to learn—and not forget—what works for the whole.

We cannot imagine our lives without blessing as a touchstone. But, as a Leading Cause of Life it goes deeper than that. Blessings have an unpredictable and even ferocious power to change the way we envision life and ourselves. Because we do not own them, their nature cannot be predicted.

In the biblical story of Jacob, who would have imagined that it would take wrestling with an angel in the dead of the night for him to receive a blessing, and the limp that would remind him of it for the rest of his life? Who would have imagined that a disease as destructive as alcoholism would also have the power to bless the lives of alcoholics with serenity, courage, and wisdom? Who would have imagined that once given, blessings cannot be called back?

It is perhaps inevitable that it is through our children that we best grasp both the benevolence and the ferocity of blessing. The world may be in an epic struggle with storm clouds on all sides, but the desire to affirm and protect our children leads us towards our better selves. At the same time, the blessings of children lead us to examine our lives in ways we never expected. Where did the "problem child's" problems come from? If we look closely there is little in our children that we cannot recognize in ourselves, and the blessing of family requires that we find it, name it, work with it, and move beyond the boundaries of easy expectation. Susan Briehl, who, along with Marty Haugen, wrote *Turn My Heart: A Sacred Journey From Brokenness to Healing*, tells the story of her daughter noticing that sadness had overtaken Susan's life when they lived in a valley that rarely saw the sun.[59] With uncanny accuracy, our children point out the steps we must take.

Sometimes it is life itself that gives the blessing. Think of a father and his teenage son whose relationship had grown fractious over the years. The two went sailing, perhaps trying to create the opportunity to negotiate a better relationship. A squall came out of nowhere, as squalls always do. The sail filled with wind, and its boom violently crossed the boat, hitting the father in the head and knocking him unconscious. The son, who couldn't do anything right, had to take the helm and sail out of the storm and into harbor where he could find help for his father. To the astonishment of both, he did it just fine. The son, who couldn't do anything right, did something both courageous and right; and his father received a gift that words hadn't found a way to allow. They had been blessed: that which had been incoherent became coherent; that which had been without hope found hope; that which had been disconnected became connected, and that which didn't know what to do knew what to do when the storm of blessing swept through Long Island Sound.

As Larry noted, we cannot bless ourselves. We can ask for blessing. We can give blessings to others, and we can receive them. And, because they are of life, we cannot live without them.

—m—

People in the odd and adolescent culture of the United States tend to act as if everything that ever mattered is known *now*, or soon will be. What works is what is next. That would not be so dangerous, if we actually thought very hard about that next world more than ten minutes in the future. "Nah, we'll figure it out *then*," we say.

There have only been about a thousand generations since we were recognizable as *Homo sapiens sapiens*.[60] At no point in any nuclear family is there likely to be more than three, at most four, generations ready to talk to each other. So the critical variable to "success" is whether we manage to hand down the best of memory and hope to the next set of people, thus allowing the present and future members of the web of life to continue to adapt and live. As longer-lived cultures know, a cause of sustained life is the profound sense of living in a web of blessing that includes those before, after, and all around us. I want to call that quality "blessing," but frankly the English language simply fails us here. The word "blessing" has too many quaint overtones of organized religion. I have tried (only on academic groups) to talk about "intergenerativity" which is technically closer, but utterly unintelligible to anyone actually alive. There is surely a good African word, but I don't know it yet. I'm trying to describe the kind of generative, emergent, productive process that happens across the relationships among multiple generations. The link between the generations generates. Maybe that's why they are called "generations" in the first place—so maybe English works after all. Let's stay with "blessing" and follow the trail.

Any Marxist or capitalist can map the interdependencies of critical stuff we need; they also have simplified ideas about the motivations that animate these crude exchanges. Whether we are talking about contrived consumer "needs," (I'm listening to downloaded MP3s as I write), or fundamental factors of production (I am tapping my foot to the music while sitting on what was once Cherokee land and would still be if it hadn't been "needed" by immigrant settlers). Capitalists and Marxists are smart, if not very charming, about mapping the needs and negotiations at any one snapshot in time. But their eyes glaze over when we ask about more durable human relationships. Life depends on relationships that are channels of blessing among the whole, which their minor calculations can't quite figure out. I am talking about a more fundamental life issue—the flow between generations that sustains the life of all of us now and of those to come.

This is anything but academic. This is the real issue UNICEF faces when confronting 20 million vulnerable children who obviously need an answer that nurtures their life over the time it takes to grow a person—about a generation. This is the question that confronts anyone responsible for thinking through a long-term organizational strategy, whether it is a church, hospital, or university. It is the question in the eyes of the elders as they watch the young getting married, and why parents' grief is so inconsolable when they lose a child.

We need what we already have—a deep sense of the primal need to be a blessing to those who come behind us, and a deep sense of accountability to those who have come before. This relationship does not feel merely mechanical and functional, but has some sense of mystery, of what I want to call blessing. This sense of blessed connection extends to those who are not yet here and those who are already gone. Any African would say, "What do you mean 'not here'; what do you mean, 'gone'?" What we in the West characterize as ancestor worship is simply the acknowledgment that those who have gone before are still among us in ways that are tangible, and that our ancestors deserve honor. African cultures have highly evolved ways of ritualizing the deep sense of accountability inherent in that acknowledged presence. Like anyone else's religious ritual, it can seem superficial and contrived to those of us on the outside. (I can't imagine how hard they would have to look to find something interesting in one of our normal church services.) Acting with a daily sense of honor for the generations extending before and after us is far more likely to generate sustained life than a life that is collapsed totally onto its own brief years. A consciousness that sees the generations before and after our own is smarter than the false autonomy based on the worship of the present.

> We need what we already have—a deep sense of the primal need to be a blessing to those who come behind us, and a deep sense of accountability to those who have come before.

—⚍—

If blessing was only a consciousness of those before us, it would be profoundly conservative, a drag on adaptive innovation that would have selected our species out of the competition many hundred generations ago. Blessing is the dual consciousness extending before and after us. This consciousness results in gratitude and responsibility that is life giving, life causing. It makes the species fit in exactly the way Salk was hoping for since it helps us to adapt, to exploit the opportunities of the new environments and thrive. Salk noted that evolution is an error-making process that finds creativity in the random mistakes that provoke corrections that from time to time surpass the original. A mistake provokes an innovative correction, which turns out to be *fit*.[61] That happens at every level of life from cells to societies. Blessing gives us enough contexts to recognize really big mistakes that would otherwise not be felt in any one lifespan, such as those that are contributing to the warming of the Earth. And blessing is the quality that seeks life that bridges terrible mistakes with a sense of accountability to those that come long after them.

My parents, Roy and Beatrice, both passed on some years ago, first dad and then mom in 1998. They lived long and worthy lives, an engineer and an educator who poured hours beyond hours into every Methodist church they joined. Rarely do I make it to ten o'clock on any morning without thinking of them and their continued affect on my life. I wonder if my dad would be proud of me, and I act differently as I reflexively sense the answer. I smile when I recognize a behavior in myself in which my mother's life can be traced. As I write this, I recall that she told me near her death that she had taught me everything she could, and that I would remember it when I needed to. To call them "lessons" is too simplistic. They gave me, in their different ways, a sense of being blessed and wanting to be worthy of it. I had a friend from Burkina Faso who graduated from the University of Georgia with a Ph.D. in agriculture and, to everyone's amazement, returned home to his rural province. He was amazed that we were amazed. "When I die," he said, "I want to come before my father and say, 'Here is what I did with my life.' I hope to be worthy of his blessing." So do I, and it shapes how I live.

Likewise, as a parent with daughters, I often reflect on whether they are proud of how I am living, of the choices I am making with my time and talent. This includes, but is far more than, what I am doing for *them* at the moment. I am sure that as a mostly normal American middle-class father I do far more materially than is good for them or the planet. I am thinking of something more basic: Am I living so that they will feel they are blessed by my life in its

> **Blessing is the dual consciousness extending before and after us. This consciousness results in gratitude and responsibility that is life giving, life causing.**

125

wholeness, not by the stuff I give or the privileges I make possible? Have I helped them to be fully alive? This is true in the immediate time when they are young, but even more as I anticipate how they will view me when I take my father's place and they take mine in the web with their own son or daughter. Will I have played my role in the web of blessing that is life itself?

What more tangible question could I ask with more concrete implications? Compared to the simplistic arithmetic of Marx or Adam Smith, the question of blessing illuminates and explains much more of what actually matters. It explains the otherwise irrational patterns of altruism and sacrifice that are quite normal among humans, although we always seem surprised when it blossoms. Think of the honor among soldiers or the always astonishing, but utterly predictable, generosity of the poor. Think of the kindness to strangers without which any city from Bangalore to Bangor would devolve into jungle. I've been in some of the most troubled human habitations on the planet—I'm thinking of Lagos and Port au Prince—so I know it is prudent to beware of the ever-present urban dangers. But even there I have learned to expect hospitality, kindness, and humor—the qualities of blessing that are present wherever humans gather. This generative behavior is caused by something other than calculation.

Some behavioral researchers imagine elaborate feedback loops of subtle interest and advantage to explain altruism as if it was as exotic as a quark. I think the life in us causes it. We are alive because life has made us this way; we are this way because we need to be for recognizable human life to go on. It is what works, at least for humans.

My description of blessing may focus too much on images of family and their blood links across generations. Something like blessing causes life in non-blood relationships too, even in what we think of as business environments. The Interfaith Health Program trains teams of leaders to think of at least a half-generation vision for their community.[62] This helps persons who are too familiar with immediate pain and too good at responsive planning to think in a different time span. Almost nothing truly transformational can happen in less than half of a generation, at least not involving humans. Almost any problem can be turned in that amount of time, however.

What school system could not imagine basic change in 14 years? The One Campaign can tell you pretty accurately what it would cost to cut global poverty in half in less time than that.[63]

Fear is rarely clever or creative enough to solve any very big problem. Fear is great at separation, but terrible at connection.

A half-generation is a long time and a short time—a real time to which we can be accountable. Even in our obsessively "now" culture, we can think that far ahead. The trick is to see the energy for blessing—not just fear—that we might be able to recognize and draw on. The instinct at city or global levels is to jack up the decibels of fear, trusting only our short-term anxiety to move us through. Surely the energy that draws us forward is as powerful as that which drives us back. Fear is rarely clever or creative enough to solve any very big problem. Fear is great at separation, but terrible at connection. There must be another basic stream of causation likely to generate the adaptive capacities that rest on creativity, sacrifice, and hope for the future.

—⚏—

Where can you find blessing? Look for the other Leading Causes of Life and you'll see it. Where you see agency being expressed between generations, you'll find persons filled with a deep sense of being blessed, and blessing that just seems like common sense to each of them. They'll be a bit taken aback to have themselves named as something that sounds so noble and cosmic. Heroes always seem a bit surprised by themselves: "I did what anyone would do." It just seems like what they *have* to do, which is the whole point. It is normal, not extraordinary or exotic. It is normal to find people acting sacrificially and tenderly to the young; normal in the same way that the very young act kindly to the aged. We should expect to find that the grandmothers on the meanest streets would go into danger on behalf of the kids for whom no one else seems to have any hope. Only those locked into the mindset of rational exchange could miss blessing or fail to expect it. You'll notice how tightly linked the blossom of blessing is to the sense of connection, and how most strong systems of coherence build a web of meaning across generations with their symbols and most powerful stories. You'll notice how our desire to be agents of blessing motivates the deepest reserves of agency, far beyond those justified by rational self-interest. Isn't that what you'd expect life to do?

CHAPTER SEVEN
Hope

Hope is the cause that shows up in every small group we've ever gathered to talk about life. It is the one with the richest library of documentation in every possible discipline. Hope is a theological lodestone attracting the most profound of every generation of every faith.

Of all the five Leading Causes of Life, only one requires an adjective if we are to discern its true meaning. That cause is *hope*. And the adjective is "informed." Informed hope is a leading cause of life. Wishful thinking will not suffice. Optimism devoid of reality can bring us both to denial and despair. But informed hope is grounded in life itself. It is not an event. It is a process. It is not afraid of discouraging facts. It knows that magical thinking is often an escape from life whereas informed hope is of life. Informed hope has a way of saying, "Yes, these untoward events have happened, and there is no way to turn back time. But you still have a life to live. Live it!"

I write of informed hope, not false hope, because it has sustained me through more than half a century of Type 1 diabetes. As a child I read about a cure for diabetes that was just around the corner, but soon realized that if waiting for a cure meant waiting for my life, my hope would be misplaced. Little did I know how deep the search for informed hope would be when I became a husband and father.

My wife, Connie, and I have four children—three sons and a daughter, each of whom has inherited her chronic and crippling bone disease. Although movement causes pain, they live life with stunning intensity and great courage, only to find at the end of each day that their pain remains. To think of hope in their lives as wishful thinking or heroic escape would diminish its sustaining presence and power.

"Hope would not be relevant were it not for the despair waiting in the wings," Connie writes. "There is never free and clear hope. It is tinged with the bittersweet shadow of despair waiting, waiting for its turn in the cycle between the two. Each gives the other meaning. We don't trust the cliché stories about 'hope as victory' because we know better. We know there is no such thing as free hope, just as there is no such thing as an eternal, cloudless, clear blue sky. The clouds come back. And they, too, are grand."

Hope needs all the friends it can find and, not surprisingly, many of them are to be found in the other Leading Causes of Life. The search for a doctor who would partner with our children and Connie as their condition progressed became a search for hope that would not be constrained by the narrow connotations of cure. Frequently it was a frustrating search leading to dashed expectations. One day our family doctor told us about a new orthopedic doctor in a nearby town. Having nothing to lose, I thought it would be worth calling her and setting up an appointment.

"I would just like to speak with the doctor," I said to the receptionist. "The situation is complicated and I really don't want to bring a million x-rays. I just want to talk with her, to meet her, after that we'll find time for the x-rays." My words fell on reluctant ears, and it soon became apparent that the

receptionist did not want to schedule such an unusual re-
quest. Cynicism made me wonder if there isn't a billing code
when a father or husband just wants to interview a doctor
about the meaning of healing and the practice of medicine.
It was as though only technology could crack the scheduling
code. But finally the flustered nurse scheduled a time for the
conversation. When the day finally came, I met with the doctor, and we talked over a cup of coffee about my family.

What was I looking for?

I was searching for a voice of hope utterly devoid of the
heroic, unfettered from wishful thinking, and unbound by
optimistic expectations. I was not in search of a miracle
worker. In most cases neither time nor life allows for that.
Instead, I was in search of informed hope. The goal was not
to have her say, "Yes, I can cure that." The goal was to see if
we could establish a relationship open to hope, a relationship that cared about life.

A poster on the wall of a Billings, Montana, neurologist
frames it well from the physician's point of view.

> The good physician knows his patients through and
> through—and this knowledge is bought dearly.
> Time, sympathy, and understanding must be lavishly dis-
> pensed, but the reward is to be found in that personal
> bond which forms the greatest satisfaction of the practice
> of medicine.
> One of the essential qualities of the clinician is interest in hu-
> manity, for the secret of the care of the patients is in
> caring for the patient.
> — Anonymous

Such a relationship both creates and sustains informed
hope that allows the living of life to be our primary task.

Larry

—◊◊—

Hope strong enough to cause life thrives in the connections
and separations that frame our most basic human experience. Greg

Fricchione, the psychiatrist that helped us understand the primal basis of connection as a cause of life, also shows how basic hope is to the human way of life.[64] The future is as real for humans as the past is for other kinds of animals. Indeed, the future may well be more powerful in that it can draw us together into taking great risks and facing great dangers because of the prospect of life beyond the present fears. The future draws us as if we remember it already happening. This is called the "memory of the future," a phrase coined by David Ingvar in 1985.[65] Fricchione links hope to connection: there is no such thing as autonomous, solitary hope

> **Hope strong enough to cause life thrives in the connections and separations that frame our most basic human experience.**

found among humans. This raises the stakes very high, since we are anxious about future threats to those we love. The more we consider the future, the more expansive and connected our hope must be.

I am writing these particular paragraphs on an airplane flying toward New York on the very day that everyone who can read a newspaper or watch a TV has been immersed in the stew of a new terror plan to blow up planes like mine with liquid bombs. It turns out that I am connected to people who want to kill, destroy, devastate, and terrorize. Today we are connected in fear. Is there any hope that we might be connected, someday, in *life* too? Hard to imagine, but the more complex the fear, the more complex the hope that we need will be. The hope that gives us life is not wishful thinking that ignores the cancer, the extinction of entire species, or bitter cries of anger and humiliation. It is a hope with eyes wide open, perhaps even with a breaking heart that still finds a hint of a memory of what might yet be. A hint of a hope is enough to draw us together so that we can begin to notice connections that can give us life. We notice choices that lead toward life, not away from it. Those choices feel like remembering something that is there to be found.

Hope is so uniquely human, and its consequences so powerfully appreciated, that it is wise to continue the section on hope by noting that it is also the most dangerous. If untethered from the other causes, it can get any group of humans overextended in ways that more thoughtful mammals would avoid. I'm thinking of the 16th-century peasants who sought to overthrow the coalition of princes who had decided to stop the radical drift of the Reformation. The princes particularly disliked those ideas based on the parts of the Bible that clearly sided with the poor against the rich (which are so numerous they were difficult to miss once the Bible was printed and available beyond the castles). Martin Luther, always the practical one with hope firmly in self-control, sided with the princes against the theological radicals that scared him too.[66] The peasant army gathered for battle with mixed feelings. To their great misfortune a brilliant morning rainbow suddenly arced through the sky. They took this (who wouldn't?) as a sure sign of their impending victory. Even though they had a rainbow, the princes had a real army. Thus, filled with hope against hope, they marched out to their predictable slaughter. Hope isn't always a pathway to life, especially when religious symbolism is driving the bus too fast around the curve.

—⁂—

Hope—connected, coherent, grounded in agency, and expressing blessing—is a wondrous engine of life to behold. William and Diane Young are pastors of The Healing Place, down near the airport in South Memphis. William was the first African American chaplain hired at Methodist Healthcare, which only happened back in the 1980s; and he is well known as a mental health professional. If I had known him when I was writing *Boundary Leaders*, he would have been on the cover. He moves with grace across every possible boundary that others still find impenetrable. He has a call-in radio show that has aired at 6:30 A.M. every Sunday for the past 12 years. People call in for prayer, and William prays for them right across the boundaries of their fears, right there on the air. Politicians call in for prayer, as do mothers for their incarcerated sons, members for their pastors, and many people for their "nerves" (which William knows is code for depression and other mental illnesses). And then he goes off to lead a day full of church with his wife, Diane. Hope is what emerges from this complicated dance. And hope is what drives it, too. Or maybe hope is what pulls it forward—for Diane and

William see something coming where others only see things failing to come at all. Hope here is both fruit and root. Emily Dickinson wrote "hope is a thing with feathers."[67] Diane and William give it wings.

More than a hundred kids come to church at The Healing Place and, wow, do they need prayer. Diane gives them hope too. She knows the children by name, not by type, so she knows that most of them are individuals with an array of skills and capacities. She sees that they are like any kids in any school: these kids are smart, curious, and capable of succeeding.

Most of the kids in Memphis schools face a tough and lonely walk through the valley of the shadow of failure. About a third never graduate from high school. But what if the lives of these kids were not on their own? What if they were not left to be distracted? They would probably be on the honor role, Diane calculated. And that is what she announced, as if it was a memory of something that had already come to be, a memory of the future. She didn't just announce her hope and sit back to watch. Rather, her hope for the kids moved her to find the 36 schools in which her kids are scattered. And then she got in her car and into the principal's office of every one of those schools. The astonished school administrators listened as she said that every one of the church's kids was going to be on the honor role. If they showed any sign of not doing so, she wanted to hear about it. If any of them gave anyone in the school any trouble, she really wanted to hear about that as well.

A pastor is a shepherd, and these young sheep had places to go and things to accomplish. They were not on their own. If their mom was in jail, somebody else in the church would be there for Parents' Night. If the kids had homework, someone would get them to the church to study. If they got in trouble—though they better not—the pastor would be there to pick them up. That is hope with an edge—the kind of hope that life would have evolved to help humans when they had little else to work with. That's the kind of hope you'll find if you know to look for it and work with it.

Every mammal has a memory of the past that helps it avoid making the same mistakes twice. Dogs learn their human family members' most subtle behaviors. My dog, Henry, knows that walking shoes mean he might get to go walking, and that basketball shoes do not. This makes him very smart about things that have happened to him before, but not so smart about things that have never happened, and might not, during his lifetime. Humans uniquely have that sort of intelligence, what Greg Fricchione earlier referred to as a "memory of the future."[68] Humans tend to live out of their expectations, not just their histories. We anticipate, expect, weigh the likelihood, and then act as if that is what is unfolding. Where my dog Henry maps the future from the past, we can do nearly the opposite. We map the present from the future, and then use that map to get there. For Diane the idea that her kids could be honor students was so vivid, it was as if it had already happened. So she got in the car and did what that memory demanded of her. The future is in many ways more real than the past or present in that it has the power to claim her time, attention, resources, and energy. She remembers, so she acts. And how could you miss all the other causes of life set loose in the process? The direct, tangible connections her hope made with the schools, so often left on their own except when blame is due. Connecting her kids connects the schools and the educators in them. The coherence celebrated in The Healing Place is visible in the most broken places making the worship a celebration of something visible, not just something desperately begged for. Agency is all over this—in the kids actually doing their homework, church members doing extra parenting, preachers showing up in places nobody expects. The generations care for each other and you can begin to see the arc of history turning just a bit more toward justice, just as Dr. King saw happening. Dr. King was remembering the future of his people, the mountaintop visible to him before the rifle shots sang out taking him, but not his memory, just a couple miles north of The Healing Place. It's a long walk from here to that mountain, one measured in generations. But with hope, we'll get there. That's what life does. Bet on it.

Hope is a "riskable" expectation. Memories of the past are slippery and uncertain and so are these expectations. They work only when tested against the memory of the group to which you are most connected (or at least your wife's memory, is my advice). Memories of the future are most viable when tested against the hopes of others that may be connected to you in ways that might not be obvious. Fricchione and others link this kind of memory to altruism and the mystery of selfless love. It certainly goes beyond the simplistic calculation needed for immediate exchange of goods and services. Humans need way more for life. I can't recall ever wanting anything from an Eskimo, but the shared horizon made visible by global warming connects us in a way that compels me to pay attention: driving my cars melts their ice. I share a future, if not a past, with people affected by my actions. Our hopes are entangled and even more so when we think of being in the same web of blessing for those who will come after us. What does life ask of us? What does life make possible for us? Do we also have shared agency? Could we find a shared memory of the future to live into now? If we can, it will be one that calls us to adapt to circumstances none of our ancestors could advise us about, other than to continue hoping for those who will follow. Don't give up. Don't tear the web of blessing. Hope—then act.

—⚌—

Frances Moore Lappé and her daughter Anna Lappé wrote *Hope's Edge* a generation after Frances' book *Diet for a Small Planet* sold millions of copies.[69] Frances' book reflected her young shock of the unnecessary hunger in the world and its link to our diet. *Hope's Edge* is a different book that models the way that we get hope from our kids, even as we try to give it to them. This mother-daughter team realized their hope did not appear to be in the same weight class as the dominant ideas about the global economy. Economists mock those who protest the dominant drift as "warriors in the struggle between the forces of global capital and something-or-other." The Lappés realized that the main voices of our time "cannot envision anything beyond today's world, in which multinational corporations, largely unaccountable private entities, wield more power than do elected governments. They cannot see what has been emerging in three decades: the innovations in creating communities that tap nature rather than squander it and ensure community, not division."[70] So off the women went to trace their memory of the future across five continents and into a new coherence woven from the threads discovered on the ground. Hope to connections, connections to agency, agency to coherence, which illuminates blessing. This chain of causes may not be enough or in time. Who is to say? But what is happening is what you would expect to happen if life causes life the way we are proposing. You can see it everywhere you look, if you know what you're looking for. It looks like life finding a way.

The well-lived life is not delusional, but the opposite. It is one informed by a hope for those things that matter the most: the ones to whom one is connected the most. It is grounded in a sense of possible choices that could bend the curve toward life, especially the life that would endure beyond one's own.

Times of frightful transition, such as our own, call out those who steal the hopes of some in order to claim it for themselves. They use their agency to steal rather than bless, which at the very least undermines the life of the whole. Garrison Keillor writes in the introduction to his collection of poetry *Good Poems for Hard Times*, "The beloved country awash to the scuppers in expensive trash, gripped by persistent jitters, politics even more divorced from reality than usual, the levers of power firmly in the hands of a cadre of Christian pirates and bullies whose cynicism is stunning, especially their perversion of the gospel of the Lord to blast the poor and meek and subvert the tax system in favor of the rich, while public institutions are put into perceptual financial crisis . . . ."[71] One gasps for breath and wonders what to do. Keillor says that when "this spirit is betrayed by the timid and the greedy and the naïve, then we must depend on the poets."[72] If we have true words, we are not all lost. Life will take it from there.

Deitrich Bonhoeffer, writing from a Nazi prison, stared directly into the cold-blooded lunacy of evil.[73] He died days before WWII ended in one of Hitler's final acts of meaningless vengeance, so we have no idea what he would have said as an old man. As a young one Bonhoeffer built that most wonderful of all human creations: a community of seekers who gathered every day to read Scripture and talk about what it called on them to do in the real world. It was a seminary, as despised by the German church as it was by the government, because it showed that there was a way other than death and fear. The community of prayer brought them into deep and compelling connection to each other, in which they could imagine, as clearly as a memory, the kind of world God was creating out of the broken and bent pieces of the world all around them. They were most fully alive dancing in the jaws of death. And who is to say they were naïve? A generation after they died, their words powered others through the darkest days of South African apartheid to see the most progressive constitution on the planet emerge peacefully. Two generations later, our lives draw life from the ones they laid down. We are more coherent, and our agency finds encouragement, from their sacrifice. We are blessed and want to bless others with similar courage and wisdom. They hoped and we are linked in their web of blessing to act.

Here you see how inseparable the Leading Causes of Life are from each other, the ensemble in the full bloom of life—especially in the way it is capable of giving life across and beyond boundaries of blood, race, class, and language. The hope that emerged—and still does—was anything but private. This hope trusted in the life of the whole that would persist, even triumph, in other lives to follow.

Hope tells us what to do, not just what to wait for. It empowers the search for coherence; it doesn't replace it. It brings us together, not apart. It allows us to see a larger story in which we can find our own more personal one. When we meet on Thursday mornings with small groups of pastors to talk about their lives, it is striking how often hope is relatively dim and silent. This generation of clergy, from almost all denominations, has health indicators that rank them among the most unhealthy professions in the country. In Bonhoeffer's time it was the opposite, clergy being among the most long-lived professionals on the planet. Despite our recent decade of hyper Christianity, the clergy we see are part of a tradition that seems to be in decline. The United Methodist Church has shrunk every one of its past 39 years.[74] While still the second largest Protestant denomination in the nation, with just under eight million members, its clergy sense a long, slow drift into irrelevance.[75] Those tending John Wesley's hope today find themselves unsuccessful at turning the decline, and they internalize the failure. Nobody can really say

> **Hope tells us what to do, not just what to wait for. It empowers the search for coherence; it doesn't replace it. It brings us together, not apart. It allows us to see a larger story in which we can find our own more personal one.**

that the extra forty pounds on the average clergy person (I am being gentle here) are attributable to the loss of Christendom. It is a bit unfair to blame Christendom's passing on these people, as if lousy sermons brought the whole thing down. Fred Smith points out that it is unhealthy to be among the first generation of clergy serving in post-Christendom. This turns out to be so.

> **The point of this book is to say that it is premature to give up on the care-giving enterprise (although good wine is still a good idea). Hope is the only antidote relevant to fear.**

It is important to note that nurses aren't so healthy these days. Neither are doctors, social workers, inner city elementary school teachers, pastoral counselors, and a long list of other caring types of people.[76] It turns out it's a dangerous time to care for others.

The antidote for the poor health of caring persons is not psychotropic pharmaceuticals, although most laypersons would be surprised to learn that we provide them to our clergy by the barrel. Jogging, vegetables, and tofu wouldn't hurt, but seem unlikely to get to the root. The whole question of looking for the problem only turns up a long and depressing list of risk vectors. What are the life vectors? Is there any hope, or should we just collapse into ourselves, turn up our iPods, and buy the best wine we can while the earthship goes down.

The point of this book is to say that it is premature to give up on the care-giving enterprise (although good wine is still a good idea). Hope is the only antidote relevant to fear. Thus we better not pretend to hope. Every pretense is transparent to those trying to care for persons up close where you can smell the sweat, see the tears, and measure the losses daily. Caregivers are most vulnerable because they are most exposed to the toxic foolishness of pretense.

We look for hope where it matters most. We look in the lives of those to whom we are connected. We look for it where persons gather on the edge of incoherence to find meaning, song, ritual, and, yes, poetry that sprouts like the first tough buds through the snow. We look for it, as did the Lappés, where persons are acting as agents in their own future. We look for it, and always find it, where

Our sustained life will be caused by the connected choices we make, and the actions we take informed by common coherent meanings driven by a primal hope for those that come after us. There is no more urgent task for us than to move together with purpose and confidence toward strategies based on the logic of life.

grandmothers reach out with practical tenderness to the children and talk to them of their own future. Life finds another way—it adapts as long as we are together. That's how life works. Look around you and test your doubts against this testimony. See if it doesn't carry you toward actions worth taking on behalf of those within range of your caring, at least for another season. That is all a human gets to hope for, as our longest lives are but a season, and some much shorter than that. All the humans who have ever been have died. But life? It goes on, and it is our purpose and joy to participate in its powerful, playful generation.

We listen to the arithmetic of the warming planet, shifting ocean currents, dying forests, and ever wilder hurricanes. It seems likely that the human strategy has about done itself in. If we do manage to dance off the precipice back to safety, it will not be because we have out-analyzed the problems our thoughtlessness has created. Our sustained life will be caused by the connected choices we make, and the actions we take informed by common coherent meanings driven by a primal hope for those that come after us. There is no more urgent task for us than to move together with purpose and confidence toward strategies based on the logic of life.

CHAPTER EIGHT
Life Together

It is cold and often gray in the North Georgia Mountains on the last day of the last month of the year. I walk down their slope amid leafless trees, slipping and sliding in the loud brown leaf fall, slapped by gray branches, cut by tangled dry vines. I have come to love the winter woods for the way the land is visible, for the old logging roads crisscrossing like hard-won scars that deserve to be seen. It turns my thoughts to the lives that preceded me on these hills, lives filled with struggle. I love how every now and then, even in the slant winter sun, there is a surprise. Down amid the leaf clutter on the low moss growing on a decade-down log is a neon-red tendril reaching up. No poinsettia forced to bloom in church, this slender stem thrust up and out like bold red boots in a biker bar. Suddenly, as my mind turns from last season to the next, I can almost feel the life surging through the roots beneath my boots. Life waits, but not for long. Winter is the pause—spring is the point. It is there to see, everywhere, all the time.

I have come to expect to find life even amid the most intractable problems. But how can we keep our concentration on life when there is such pressure to drift back into the melancholy majority that works away on death? The answer is found in the multiple meanings of the simple word "discipline."

"Discipline" is the word we give the work of concentration when an individual is trying to stay focused on a task over a period of time. The opposite of discipline is distraction. To be distracted from physical labor is to lose the sequence of tasks. To be distracted from intellectual labor is to lose the point, to wander rather than pursue the subject, to forget the tools and their purpose. A discipline can mean a set of tools and rules, but it can also mean the body of persons that share a respect for those tools and rules. I am hoping for a discipline around the Leading Causes of Life that results in a web of relationships among persons working on life in similar ways. I want a life discipline in both senses.

Sometimes discipline comes to mean a way of living, such as *The Book of Discipline* of The United Methodist Church, which more or less captures the way of life John Wesley urged upon his radical religious movement. That movement is now tempered and tamed by becoming a large Protestant religious enterprise, but the idea at its heart speaks to a profound focus on the love of God that could bind a large community to its purposes. The book is revised every four years by the conference of his followers called United Methodists— sometimes advancing his ideas, sometimes drifting off toward other less radical ways of doing things. *The Book of Discipline* provides some fences to guide the process as it reminds the current cohort of followers where they came from and the rules of engagement.

Sometimes a body of intellectual practice becomes stable enough to be known as "a discipline." It evolves into a fellowship of thinkers who do not necessarily hold the same conclusions, but pursue a way of thinking enough to be recognizable to each other. The discipline develops trustworthy tools that, if used competently even by persons one does not personally know, are likely to produce work that is recognized by and trusted by others in its field. An epidemiologist anywhere in the world uses the same basic tools as every other epidemiologist and will be recognized by how conclusions are reached based on how well the discipline was followed.

Disciplines are stable, but not entirely static. They evolve as the cumulative practice moves along a path determined by the tools of the shared discipline. Of course, sometimes the tools take over. The discipline forgets the question that generated the tools in the first place. The discipline of Public Health was once a social movement animated by the idea of systematically identifying health risks to the whole population in order to stop disease and prevent it from spreading.[77] The powerful question at the heart of the public health movement in its early years was about social patterns and political choices that could illuminate the common pursuit of health. It was a social movement that over the years devolved into a more narrowly focused set of services that were provided by the public sector, such as immunization or food inspection. One could argue, successfully I think, that the tools for pharmaceutical intervention and statistical pattern recognition of pathology gained power, while the tools for social mobilization and democratic policy development were gradually left aside. I would not want worse drugs and sloppy data. But one wishes for some sort of balance.

The problem is that Public Health as an intellectual discipline has come to be too much about problems. So have nearly all other *problem*-solving fields of practice. Nearly every other field has allowed its identity to be shaped by the problems it addresses. Training of leaders, prioritizing of work, and shaping of the annual gatherings are all dominated by the problems around which we build our identity.

We must have a new discipline, a new life together.

Let us acknowledge that a discipline formed around life is likely to be messy. Life requires some level of disrespect for the boundaries of many existing disciplines, so we can borrow from many in order to construct a new whole. Indeed, in calling for a new discipline, we encourage each other to reject existing boundaries of thought. It takes a new discipline to look toward our margins—not to the old core—for our guidance.

We are not discarding the work of the existing disciplines, just saying that the most useful parts of their work lie on their boundaries where they can lend and gain strength from other fields in a disciplined way.

Every time I have ever spoken about the Leading Causes of Life, someone in the audience has come up afterward to tell me about a group on the edges of their discipline they recognize as working on life. I have come to expect that in any possible group of people life is trying to happen—that is what it does, that is how we live. But to a remarkable degree all of these life discourses remain on the margins of their own field.

Currently anyone trying to do community-scale work on any issue of consequence to any sector or discipline finds herself or himself almost paralyzed by the lack of bridge-building, positive language, and logic. This is true partly because nearly every sector is dominated by its own problem-solvers, which focus on fixing broken things as understood by their own way of thinking. Educational problem-solvers (treating children as risks), business organizations (treating entrepreneurship as besieged by problems), religious leaders (treating persons as essentially depraved), hospitals and public health departments (treating persons and communities as always at risk of disease) all sound more and more like governments (which increasingly view most of their own citizens, and all of the rest of the planet, as risks or threats). The varied "problem-solving languages" are mutually unintelligible due to their conflicting models of precision. They all point in slightly different directions away from common life to focus on a particular kind of threat. Even the most obvious commonalties—between physical and mental health, for instance—are seldom bridged even intellectually, much less in practice, and even less at the point of policy. The groups built on these increasingly autonomous languages become more specialized and inwardly focused, as they find it hard to talk to, much less work with, other disciplines.

And yet, on the boundaries of each and every one of the fields, there is a lively discourse about life. At least, that is what the subject is once you know how to recognize it. A bit like the red fungi amid the mountain leaf clutter, you have to know to look down and around with expectation that life is going to find a way.

The first act is imagination. When I first started thinking about the Leading Causes of Life, I imagined that there might be a few glimmers in a handful of professional fields or academic departments. Now, it seems that life has been quietly subverting problem-oriented fields of all kinds—rather like you would expect life to do.

Almost every field has a life discourse on its margins. In some cases, such as psychology, the positive discourse has moved toward the center of the field.[78] In others where you might least expect it (financial accounting), you will find a small discussion going on that turns out to be about the causes of, in this case, creativity,[79] transparency,[80] and trust[81]—all of which are qualities of life.

At some point, once the discipline of life becomes more mature, it will be common practice to see the Leading Causes of Life operating within these fields, in somewhat the same way the deductive logic of death and problem-solving is now so common. You can look in your own field of practice and you'll quickly have eyes to see it everywhere.

—⚅—

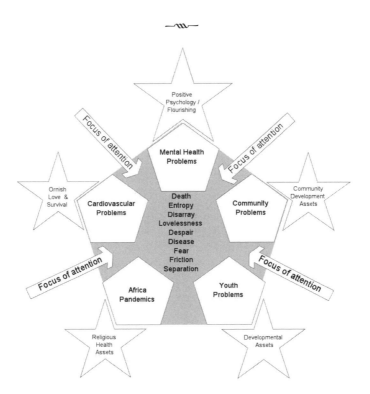

By focusing on the causes of death and a particular issue, potentially positive communities are kept distant and denied the life that may otherwise grow from them.

145

Persons are always trying to build a fellowship around a pre-ferred disease, such as one of the cancers, obesity, violence, racism, diabetes, sexually transmitted diseases, mental illness, poverty, or one of any number of environmental destructions underway. The names and images of suffering and decay currently dominate any and all of these; they are dominated by the search for strategies of engaging, preventing, and ameliorating the brokenness they de-scribe. Pathology-oriented groups tend to become support groups, ever more tightly wrapped around their shared problem.

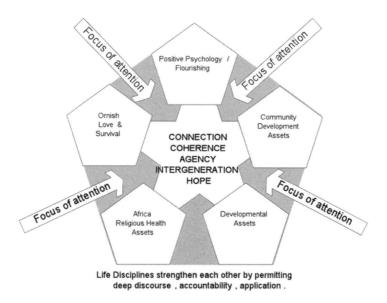

Life Disciplines strengthen each other by permitting deep discourse , accountability , application .

By focusing on the causes of life, Life Disciplines strengthen each other by encouraging deep discourse, accountability, and applica-tion.

Life wants a different way of being together, a way in which we are pulled toward each other and at the same time toward transfor-mation. The Interfaith Health Program has come to describe that new way of being together as "webs of transformation" which fits the Leading Causes of Life perfectly.[82] We knew that the only per-sons who could do *community* transformation were those working on their *own* transformation. They were drawn toward each other because of their hope for both the transformation of community and of self. That is simply the way life works. A web forms around some functional kind of connection based on a shared project. Then life starts to spin and weave, so a shared meaning emerges, and agency expresses itself beyond what all involved expected. By now you know to expect to see the whole ensemble dancing. At least it goes on when the ones nurturing the web act in ways that nurture life and don't dumb it down into a less adaptive form of structure. It is the great hope of this book that you will be able to nurture the life of the webs that form around you.

There are great pressures to let the web turn into something more common, a coalition that lives on the energy of its fear and then competes with the other fears. A food bank, for example, lives off hunger and competes for the attention of Kroger supermarkets in order to get them to be the visible sponsor for their holiday food drive. Habitat for Humanity hopes for the attention of Home Depot. About every decade some African debacle makes it into public view. The issue teams then compete like desperate candidates for public attention, sympathy, and financial support. These organizations "win" by having their problem "win": Diabetes usually loses to cancer; children's cancers win against those of the aging unless it is likely to affect mothers, who compete pretty well with the young; hunger beats homelessness, which beats anything African. As the competition is really one among varieties of fear, the fears magnify. The sum is dramatically less than the accumulated separate fears.

The powerful market for new kinds of pathologies discovers new varieties of diseases every week. Every disease and every fear creates a business for somebody or some organization. It is no wonder we hardly notice the growing life among us. In our modern cities we have become so afraid of the dark, and each other, that we keep inventing ever-brighter lights. The fear spreads even into our North Georgia mountain community. A few miles from the wilderness outside my cabin a new gas station was just built that is so brightly illuminated that it simply must be visible from space. And the galaxies that witness to a universe of wonder and delight become just a bit harder to see.

Of course, each of these individual pathologies—cancer or bioterror—derives its strength from a common pool of primal fears: death, entropy, disarray, lovelessness, despair, disease, fear, separation, and confusion. These focus our attention and dominate our imagination. It takes discipline to avoid the vortex that spins us into the center of fear.

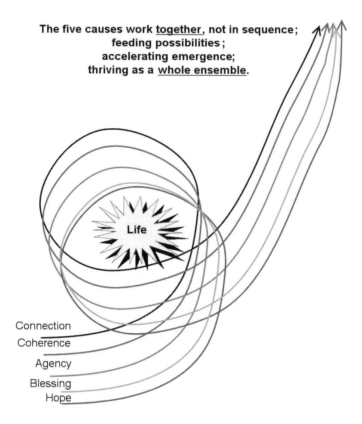

The five causes work <u>together</u>, not in sequence; feeding possibilities; accelerating emergence; thriving as a <u>whole ensemble</u>.

Life

Connection
Coherence
Agency
Blessing
Hope

Ironically, the focus of attention on death looks right past the emerging life logic growing on the margins of each of our disciplines. The causes of life are the opposite of suffering. They create fellowships that muddle the teams, sowing confusion among the competing groups. Life finds commonalties amid great complexity and drives us toward shared meaning and hope.

Imagine that instead of death, entropy, confusion, separation and so on being the focus of our attention, we concentrated in a disciplined way on seeing the life that causes growing among us. What if the currently marginalized positive discourses were no longer on the edge out of sight, but served as lenses to focus our attention on connection, coherence, agency, blessing, and hope? You will have noticed by this point that what seems like competing problems are only competing with each other for the funds and attention needed to *treat* them. It is hard to figure out how to pay for treating all the varieties of death. But many

> **Imagine that instead of death, entropy, confusion, separation and so on being the focus of our attention, we concentrated in a disciplined way on seeing the life causes growing among us.**

pathologies are prevented using identical activities, which are recognizable as strategies of life. Diabetes, stroke, hypertension, smoking, teen pregnancy, even erectile dysfunction are all *prevented* by life strategies that get us to exert our agency and encourage each other to walk around the block.[83] When the Bishop of the Iowa Conference of The United Methodist Church convinced many of the clergy to drink eight glasses of water every day, walk 10,000 steps, and read the Bible every day, the increase in insurance costs stopped cold for four years in a row. Walking and reading the Bible are strategies of life that tend to compete pretty well with disease if you give life some encouragement across connections that matter. It is one thing to talk about forming fellowship amid chubby pastors in Iowa but what about the maelstrom of race, poverty, AIDS, and gender oppression killing millions in Africa? Can we imagine a web of transformation thriving there? Well, yes, in fact.

—⟋⟍—

Near the entrance to The Apartheid Museum in Johannesburg, South Africa, is a tiny sign, no more than an inch high, down low on the brick wall that simply says, "We all share the same African ancestor." Next to it is a very large picture of one particular skull known affectionately, and surely inaccurately, as Ms. Ples (*Australopithecus Africanus*). She walked a few miles from the museum about

2.8 to 2.6 million years ago. I like to think that she was guiding her small band across the grass a bit like many of our bands of boundary leaders seeking life move around in their communities too. Among other things, the museum's sign is a good example of how we can be very, very right even when we are certainly very, very wrong. Ms. Ples is not our mother, maybe not even within a quarter of a million years of her. But we have one. One.

Walking and reading the Bible are strategies of life that tend to compete pretty well with disease if you give life some encouragement across connections that matter.

When I talk about life, I feel like I rest on the authority of our mother.

Some of the most important conversations about life I have ever had have happened during the work of the Africa Religious Health Assets Program, ARHAP. Sometimes I speak, but the most powerful things happen when I listen using the discipline of life, seeking the living fellowship that was trying to find its heartbeat. Listening. In a way that's all ARHAP is—a listening project straining to hear the birdsong amid the jets, the heartbeat of life amid the cries of cruel and vastly premature death.[84] Like other public health groups I meet with, the fellowship of ARHAP always has the presence of skulls in the room with us so vividly that we have not needed to name them. They were not two million years old like those at the museum, but perhaps only a month or two buried—and not of some imaginary early hominid mother, but of sisters and cousins we loved. We were there because they urged us, like Ms. Ples I think, not to miss the point, which is life. That's what we were trying to help each other pay attention to—the African heartbeat of life.

ARHAP has tried to help each other listen for this heartbeat. We suspect that the place where it beats the loudest is the vital confluence of health and faith. And we are quite certain that we must diligently attend to the way in which this confluence is a place of emergent life—a living asset. We expect to be surprised, and are systematic about putting our ear to the place where surprise is most likely to happen. Our awkward language of "religious health assets" keeps us focused, so that we will be paying attention when the surprise happens. The whole point of the program is to understand what we have to work with our assets and how to work with them. The point that we must not miss—that we must help each other not miss—is that the assets are alive.

The Leading Causes of Life help in Africa where death has so dominated our professional imagination. We have exquisitely sophisticated ways of mapping how we die and the phenomena that kill us. We can actually rank the various pathological causes in fine detail, a remarkable intellectual enterprise so common now that we hardly marvel at it. This systematic categorization certainly helps us fight back. The Carter Center has led a vast international coalition to beat back polio and onchocerciasis (commonly called river blindness),[85] almost eliminating them from the earth.[86] Part of the power of the leading causes of death is that the act of ranking brings order to the swarm of possible bad things. Ranking focuses the mind on what to do first, second, third, and so on. We can give priority to those diseases that are most deadly, and to those for which we have relevant tools to intervene. Polio and onchocerciasis qualify in Africa, hands down.

Compared to life, of course, death is simple. Likewise, the coalitions—fellowships—that have grown around the diseases are relatively simple. Life is more complicated than death, which is why the fellowship of ARHAP is far more complex than just an inventory of problems. That's why we have to help each other listen for the heartbeat of the assets—sometimes it's hard to hear.

If I ask you to put down this book and go outside right now to find something dead, you could be back in five minutes with a most interesting assortment. On the way back in, you could probably make a pretty good guess at why that once-alive thing is now dead. It's not that hard. But if I asked you to go outside and find something alive and bring it back, everybody might not all make it *back*. Half the stuff is moving, for one thing, and the rest might bite, play with us, hide, or even try to look dead to confuse us. And some of us would surely find the life outside more interesting, vital, beautiful, or life-giving than reading a book—some of us, myself included, would probably stay outside and join life in doing whatever it was doing.

Even such a brilliantly cruel virus as HIV is dumb simple compared to the complex life it destroys.

—⚍—

Connection. Fellowships like ARHAP live because we are seeking connection, we are seeking meaning and coherence, we are seeking agency, and we are drawn to the possibility of both blessing and receiving blessing. Our hopes give us life. We are becoming more alive the more we try to study the life of these assets. This is the experience that pervades our gatherings, and why so many of us find ways to get here, stay here, and come back. This is not only good for us, but good for the work; we get smarter and more alive at the very same time.

Life is social; I "am" because we "are." We live only because we connect in squishy, warm, vital ways. Every virus, not just AIDS, exploits this connection, of course. But we must connect. And every living fellowship moves toward more and more complex, dense, layered interconnection. Everywhere we look, we see more connections. The closer we look at what would seem like simple projects—Masangane (the South African women's program caring for persons with AIDS), for example—the more we find that there is an infinite web of connections that are their life; that evoke, support, and sustain life.

Someday, of course, like every thing human—ARHAP, Masangane, and all of our projects—will die as they lose that supple capacity to weave and adapt. But another life will emerge from the same vital logic. Steve DeGruchy notes that religious health assets are fragile, unstable, and personal. But they emerge and thrive in the most amazing way. The more we understand this vital logic, the less we will fear the apparent fragility and transience. We will trust their way of coming to life, staying alive over a healthy life span, and laying down their life too. We will be able to train leaders to lead without that fear. The lack of fear is one of the life competencies that could be expected of vital leaders nurturing the life of the social organizations that spring from faith. This may be the most vital contribution that emerges from ARHAP's studies—not just knowing where stuff is, but why these living assets are alive and how they might be nurtured.

The point of ARHAP is to understand faith-forming things so surprises can be anticipated.[87] Faith-forming things network incessantly, and will do so to the exhaustion of an academic's attention span. They connect in ways that defeat our simple languages of negotiated institutional agreements. Asking, "what's the relationship?" is much more useful than, "what's the deal?"

Living connections create trust and turn out to be far more efficient, if fragile, than negotiation. This is why Masangane can get someone on treatment in three days when the government's best efforts take three months.[88] And it is why ARHAP has proven so productive and creative.

The greatest gain in system-level efficiencies that agencies seek when looking to faith partnerships lies in the mysteries of how faith groups connect. That's why we need a participatory aspect even in our mapping.[89] You can't map these connections without connecting to those who are involved. It always seems to be more than we really need to know—unless we want to *act* on what we need to know. The more we allow our own complex connections to work, the more we will understand about these living assets, and the more alive we will be.

Coherence. The second cause of life, coherence, is ARHAP's most obvious heartbeat. It is visible in our lively attraction to new words, which are tools of coherence. Ms. Ples was recognizably human because she could see that a stick could be a tool useful for some purpose other than that intended by the tree. We also move toward meaning with a voracious appetite for words, theory, typology, and tools of meaning-making, meaning-testing, and meaning-re-making. This is serious play in exactly the way that life is serious, that sex is serious. It is vital. As we listen to *Bophelo*, the word of wholeness, we find it illuminates our life, a little bit as it does for the BaSotho people. It's a great tool.

Some of the words remain vital for us while others will only serve to mark a step on the way. As in biblical tongues, we may need to be sure that some of us are present to interpret the more inspired and raw inventions. But it would help to note those that recur and seem to be capable of holding meaning long enough to carry them across boundaries.

The original idea of ARHAP was to tease scholars into engaging the "bounded field of unknowing" by writing theses and articles and books.[90] We've seen the very powerful fruit of the first seven or eight theses that have emerged under ARHAP-ian influence. They are helping us greatly, including one by Jill Oliver examining hope in the context of HIV/AIDS. We can expect that living coherence will stay messy as it continues to adapt to more complex connections expressing unexpected kinds of agency. That is the work of coherence, a work of life.

Agency. Life *works*. Faith that does not work is dead. That is so obvious to religious people that we have to remember to not let that be *the only thing* that we know. Humans that are connected in webs of meaning *work*. They make choices *to do*. The Africa Religious Health Assets Program (ARHAP) works—at least to the extent that any academics do. Making, recognizing, and mapping connections is work that expresses agency and causes life. Making up new words is work that can help or distract depending on how well the work is done. The challenge of any work you do with your head is that it might be disconnected from other kinds of work. This is the life-giving potential of the collaboration with the World Health Organization and major religious groups doing health work, because they are *way* serious about the really, really urgent work. AHRAP became more alive as we discovered that *our* agency is vital to *their* kind of agency. It is the *work* in which we will find our life. This is true for me personally, and is why I was drawn to Memphis with the Methodist Healthcare system there.

Blessing. The fourth cause of life is blessing, which speaks to the way we find life as worthy heirs of those who have come before us and as good ancestors of those to follow. As ARHAP looks carefully at those practices that engage AIDS orphans and the ways in which people pass on powerful memories, those of us noticing will also become more alive to the life that is happening within our own web of relationships. I loved watching Jill Oliver, a young scholar, and Dr. Alan Haworth, a venerable scholar. They modeled a living, multi-generational fellowship of learning. It gives me life to see the first of what will be many theses emerge from them, knowing that they will

154

go far beyond me. It gives me life to be in the presence of Alan, who shows the power of doing honorable work as he has in one Zambian university for 41 years. The more we can see our life extending forward and backward, the more alive we become.

Hope. Africans of all shades, even my own pale one, know that life follows hope. When we were first starting ARHAP it was common to ask each other, "What are you hoping for?" Sometimes this comes out as a question about what *difference* our work will make. But in a more fundamental way, our heartbeat strengthens when we are able to visualize a vivid image of a possible future that compels us to act. We help each other hope by stretching our imaginations about what is possible. We heard how rapidly communities change perception as the reality of access to ART treatment appears. As that becomes real, we can hope in quite different ways. Faith without work is dead; hope is, too. The horizon shifts. So it is no small thing to ask continually, "Are we hoping enough for what is really possible, *now*?"

> We help each other hope by stretching our imaginations about what is possible. Faith without work is dead; hope is, too.

We will live because we hope, at least if those hopes reflect our connections, coherence, agency, and place in a stream of blessing.

—⁂—

The Africa Religious Health Assets Program (ARHAP) may seem exotic and difficult to relate to, at least if you are on the committee working to get those chubby Iowa pastors to lose weight. But every group that tries to work on something life-giving could tell a similar story to AHRAP's. Its basic insight—*that assets are alive*—applies to every congregation and committee, be it secular, governmental, religious, educational, or some hybrid. It is vital for those leading these gatherings to do so using logic of life.

It takes discipline to avoid turning the Leading Causes of Life into another way of seeing what is wrong in a group. This happens when we look at our committee and realize that we can't see any sign of, let us say, hope. I'm still thinking of those church committees, obviously. The instinct is to go get some hope to stuff into the yawning gap as quickly as possible. We concentrate our attention on what we lack for fear that the weakness will collapse everything like a building on a bad foundation. Life doesn't work like a building, which is, technically, always trying to fall down, resisting gravity only because of careful design. Life, even the life of a committee, isn't trying to fall down; it's trying to live, find its way, and grow.

At times we all succumb to this temptation, usually as we ponder our lack of financial resources. "Gee, if we had more money, we'd have more agency, thus more hope, and a lot more life," goes the logic. The discipline of life insists that life begets life, thus the way to get more life is to find that which already exists and to nurture more of it.

A church committee might focus on its connections rather than leaping toward an artificially grand and imported hope. Who are we really connected to and how? The task is to appreciate and map the connections that currently define a group in order to find the rich and vital connectedness that gives it life. Who are we connected to that we don't yet see? To whom should we connect that we have missed? How can we deepen and accelerate the connections among us already involved? That will look like life, I promise.

I love connections and can never resist connecting living things to each other: hospitals to Africa, congregations to surgeons, bishops to public health workers, poets to prophets. Because I expect to find connections, I do. Memphis is not far from Missouri, a state that is proud of being the "Show Me State." It only believes what it sees. Dr. William Foege, who started the Interfaith Health Program when he was the Executive Director of The Carter Center, knows it is actually the other way around. *You only see what you believe*, so you have to be careful what you believe.[91] If you believe we live in a web of living connections, you'll see them everywhere.

—⚶—

You might think that coherence is most useful for academics and people with more time on their hands than is entirely healthy, such as executives. I just spent two weeks roaming around a United Methodist Annual Conference—the yearly gathering of all the clergy and a lot of the key laypeople doing the business of the church. This one was working on United Methodist business, but it was much the same as meetings of other denominations, changing only the particular vocabulary or peculiarities of polity. These religious gatherings are often painfully anxious and depressed, with many allusions to the better days behind them. This is especially curious considering that the church rests on an extraordinary richness of theology that is tough, smart, and tested over the centuries. You'd think it was a meeting of the shareholders of a restaurant franchise trying to market tofu in Mississippi wondering about the dismal sales figures. Wesleyan faith and logic still works way better than tofu in the South. By focusing on what they *don't* have (21st-century glitz) they forget what has been vital and life giving for a long time—their source of coherence. By not trusting what actually allows them to hold together (cohere), they long for the coercive power of structure and the distracting power of style to hold things so tightly it is hard to breathe. A little bit of focus on honest coherence might let in some fresh air and, well, life.

None of this curious lethargy is unique to Methodists. The angst is generalized among middle-aged (a couple of centuries, roughly) religious groups, not particular to theological persuasion. Religious ideas become religious movements, which gradually become religious structures, which over time create leaders who never know the thing to move at all. Movement? Salk would have no problem recognizing the process as one of a species that failed to adapt to its environment and thus was gradually selected out of the ongoing process. It wasn't fit anymore. The irony is that the ideas at the root of some of these religious structures are highly fit for the 21st century. In some ways they are fitter for the 21st than they have been for the late 20th century. John Wesley's stunningly powerful insights about ecumenical accountability groups driven by a simple commitment to love others is pretty timely. He linked spirituality to justice, mercy, and, remarkably, health. He created a non-ideological framework that respected reason, tradition, Scripture, and community that spawned both universities and a movement among the barely literate. Sounds like the latest religion to come in off the California surf. My point is that the religious movements that look most *un*-alive have at their heart a powerful transformational ensemble that may yet live again for another several generations. They are too connected to the old to recognize their vital connections to the new. But that doesn't mean they are dead or they need to die. Likewise, many clergy are overly connected to the way things are and thus feel themselves dying along with the old age that is passing. But just because the ways they have known are dying doesn't mean they need to do so. They (we) just need to focus on the flow of life. Jesus asked the fellow who has been lying at the pool for decades, "Do you want to be well?" Then show some agency, get up, and go to where the life is!

The opposite of structural lethargy is what viruses do, which is to cause epidemics. Salk imagined epidemics of *health* made possible by the same kind of simple viral contagion that spreads so adaptively in nature. What if our religious movements forgot their structure and tried to be epidemics instead?

Groups accustomed to short-term funding and vast unpromising problem solving tend to assume they can't do anything that matters very much. Pastors trapped in organizations that seem to be in a lazy death spiral feel they have no choice but to stand on the bridge and sing while the ship takes them and their families down into the cold water. It is easy to overlook the abundant agency of the group. They can move, change the subject, get a different job, switch churches, ask somebody else to join the group, pick up the phone, or get on the Web. If you can freely gather a group on an open evening, you have agency.

> The hope that matters is the one that is most vividly grounded in the connections, most resonant with your most profound meanings, most expressive of your real opportunities for agency, and most clearly appreciative of the flow of blessings alive across the generations.

What is it, and where can you get more?

Blessing sounds like something that only religious groups could do. But even in the most age-specific kind of organizations like those older men's civic groups, there is a powerful opportunity to bring to view inter-generational blessing. You just have to look. The Africa Religious Health Assets Program (ARHAP) found its blessing in the way those young students and old scholars found themselves working together on vital work. As we realized that was already happening, we focused on getting better at finding these people and supporting them in their crucial work across generations.

Finally, and perhaps most obviously, any group can talk about what it hopes for. The trick is to be disciplined about doing so in the language that moves toward life. You will have to describe hope as something more than an absence of your fears. Let the other causes of life inform your hope. The hope that matters is the one that is most vividly grounded in the connections, most resonant with your most profound meanings, most expressive of your real opportunities for agency, and most clearly appreciative of the flow of blessings alive across the generations.

This may seem like highly symbolic language to use for committee work. Don't miss the point: webs are alive. Be disciplined about how you work with life.

CHAPTER NINE
Let Your Life
Be About Life

None of us knows how long we will live. The Leading Causes of Life should help us know what to do with our lives so that we *live* at least as long as we are physically alive. A lot of people don't do that. They stare at death from decades away and let all their years be defined by the work of resisting its eventual grip. So it holds them long before it claims them. The point of the causes of life is exactly *not* longevity, at least on the personal level. The causes might or might not help you *extend* your life, but they should certainly help you deepen it and feel more useful to those you love.

Just because life is trying to happen doesn't mean we should be cavalier. It is important to follow our doctor's advice: walk a few thousand steps every day, wash our hands, floss our teeth, eat something green, and wear a seat belt. But those things won't make us more alive. The only way any of us can do that is by allowing ourselves to be

The point of the causes of life is exactly *not* longevity, at least on the personal level. The causes might or might not help you *extend* your life, but they should certainly help you deepen it and feel more useful to those you love.

more richly *connected*, to seek meaning and *coherence*, to *act* on the choices that lead to life, to extend ourselves in webs of *blessing*, and to nurture *hope* in all things. In short, the only way is to allow the causes of life to weave *in* us at the very same time they work *through us*. This is the way of life.

Not long ago, in an interview with the *Billings Gazette*, a neurologist shared the hope that new drugs can prevent strokes if the medications are received within three hours of the onset of a stroke. When the reporter asked him what would happen if the medication was not received within that time frame, he said, "There's nothing we can do." In a state like Montana where many people live at least two hours away from a hospital that might have those medicines, I read this doctor's answer with concern.

Having miraculously survived two strokes, I couldn't help but write to the newspaper, saying, "Such a comment reflects hopelessness. After all, not everyone can get to a hospital within three hours, and not all ER's know what to do when a stroke patient arrives. But rehabilitation—speech, physical and occupational therapy, together with the science of neuropsychology—provides pathways of hope for stroke patients who must rebuild their lives. Can we recover everything that's been lost? No. But can we create a new life? Yes, we often can, arduous as the process may be. Three hours, 180 minutes, can destroy our lives and our livelihood. But they cannot rob us of hope."

As I wrote the words, I knew with inner certainty that there is something non-circumstantial about hope in our lives. It may ebb, and it may flow; but hope is an inalienable quality of life.

Larry

—ɯ—

A careful examination of your own life will corroborate the presence of the five Leading Causes of Life. It will also show how the five causes work together to tell a story of marvelous complexity. Just as blue, yellow, and red are the three primary colors from which all other colors—Alizarin crimson, burnt umber, sap green, rose madder—draw their base and their translucent power, the five Leading Causes work together to paint the hues and tones of your life.

To say that all five are complete unto themselves as separate units would make for a boring painting indeed. Besides, the truth is elsewhere. Hope, for example, waxes and wanes in our lives. Hope infused with the encouragement that connection provides is a powerful thing. The often-quoted verse of Scripture that *God does not give us more than we can handle* is written not to an individual, but to a church. Or we might realize that action without connection to others could be a prescription for disaster. Niels French, one of my colleagues at the Interfaith Health Project who now works with me in Memphis, tells of African villages where well-intended drilling projects brought in new wells. The presence of more water led to more goats, which led to more foraging. It didn't take long before the larger herds overgrazed the land. What looked like a blessing turned out to be a setback for the villages' fragile ecology.

Sepetla Molapo, our Sesotho colleague who directs the African Religious Health Assets Program (ARHAP), believes coherence provides the necessary glue for the Leading Causes of Life. In his view, connection or unity leads to coherence or belonging that leads to meaning. Once shared meaning is found, trust becomes possible. And once trust is present in the equation the power of love begins to

Connection or unity leads to coherence or belonging that leads to meaning. Once shared meaning is found, trust becomes possible. And once trust is present in the equation the power of love begins to flow. Working together the five basic causes of life begin to reflect our very humanity.

flow. Working together the five basic causes of life begin to reflect our very humanity.

Larry and I can't know how life is speaking to you, but we know it is because that's what life does. The Leading Causes of Life is not a program that calls for conformity. They surface in my life quite differently than they surface in Larry's life. And they will surface in your life quite differently than they appear in either of our lives. But along the way their presence will be unmistakable.

We can't help but think of a hymn that affirms life's song:

"My life flows on in endless song;
Above earth's lamentation.
I hear the sweet though far off hymn
That hails a new creation
Through all the tumult and the strife,
I hear that music ringing;
It finds an echo in my soul—
How can I keep from singing?"

—Robert Lowry, 1860

I spend a lot of time with clergy and laypersons, sometimes focusing on their individual health and sometimes on their communities' health. It turns out to be the same subject. None of us can hope for the community by watching stories about it on TV, we have to connect. We can't hope for ourselves apart from the connections of our work, family, neighborhood, and the whole cosmos. Despair for the whole is despair for myself. Howard Clinebell, the father of pastoral counseling, noticed that among young people, their sensitivity to the destruction of the environment amplified their personal distress. He encouraged families to get involved in some hands-on project like reclaiming an abandoned lot or cleaning up a streambed—anything to experience the possibility of rebirth.[92] Hope for the whole created the possibility of hope for them. That's the way life works.

Early on in the exploration of the causes of life the work of Dr. Corey Keyes of Emory University turned on the metaphorical lights. A sociologist working mostly in the field of mental health, Keyes was doing the meticulous work of exploring the data describing the path toward or away from negative mental health. He discovered that there is not just one continuum running from terrible to terrific health, with most of us being average in the middle. Keyes showed us that there is one continuum ranging from no symptoms of mental ill health on over toward very serious symptoms and another continuum that runs from no symptoms of thriving over to what might be called abundant life. Keyes likes to talk about "languishing" as the opposite of thriving.[93] You can languish without any negative symptoms.

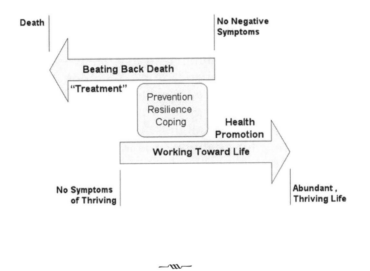

The practical implications are that there are two things to pay attention to, not just one. You simply cannot focus on helping people back away from the negative end of the spectrum by all the tools of healing and treatment you might have to apply. That is only one continuum. You simply must pay attention to the other continuum, which is to focus on those things you can do to help people along the pathway toward positive health or, dare we say, thriving. It is irresponsible to just do one without thinking about the other.

Keyes's work focuses on the mental health, but a similar logic may pertain in many other parts of health. Wherever it seems that there is a battle against death, it is highly likely that there is also a battle on behalf of life going on.

Of course, some people just take pills and hope for the best. And it would be just terrific if they worked. But pills can only slow the entropy, distracting us along the way. "I need that purple one or the little diamond shaped one then things will be okay." Life works in a different way that feels less certain. But remember that it has had a pretty good record over several billion years, many millions of which were pretty difficult. The way of life is not more arduous, fit only for heroes and geniuses. It is the opposite. Life works for any of us who follow its ways.

Always at the edges of our mind we wonder if we really should keep our minds focused on beating back death, or at least keeping it at bay. We do, after all, have abundant tools and sophisticated structures that pretty much do nothing *but* that. Do we want to distract anybody from avian flu, hurricane preparations, terrorists, teen pregnancy, or obesity? We need some folks to work on that. But we must always keep life as our primary focus.

If you are worried about all those things and the endless list of diseases competing for attention, it is more effective to work on those human characteristics that have always prevailed. One does this by nurturing our connections, enhancing our coherence, exploring our agency, holding up our capacity to bless, and finding the ground of hope.

—⚉—

Our hospital system, like nearly every one on the planet, is trying to bring the fruits of technology to bear on improving quality of care for our patients while controlling costs. Our primary technology partner for this task is Cerner, which is moving us along the pathway toward the paperless electronic record—the technical fix for all sorts of quality improvement hopes. A health system includes many moving parts: rural and urban hospitals, long-term care facilities, big-time university research hospitals, private doctors' offices, government primary care clinics, and lots of alternative providers of varied reputations. All of these have what seem like an infinite number of professional roles, each with its own language and rules.

If you can automate such a fantastically complicated, guild-ridden thing as a hospital, a community system looks relatively easy. It's not, but it seems that way looking out the window. Cerner is following the thread of patient care logic out into the community, knowing that the journey of any one patient does not *begin* at the door of the hospital. They know that the patient is a complicated person who spends all but the tiniest fraction of their days outside the health care system and certainly outside the hospital. Once you start you have to fix the whole system. The system that focuses on preventing disease and injury is most visibly the public health agencies, which themselves are multi-faceted and getting more so in the age of global risks from birds and hostile humans. The *public health* system rests on a constant and dynamic monitoring and learning network that is supposed to quickly inform public policies and then enforce them. Some of this is very mundane, such as ensuring that your local restaurant employees wash their hands. Some monitoring can be quite exotic such as when a brand new virus, like SARS, appears in China and then suddenly in Toronto. Part of the system is finding and training people who can do all these kinds of things. The *financial* system that pays for the health monitoring and learning network is bizarre, at least in the United States. Most parts of the health system spend at least as much of their creative time figuring out how to get paid as they do thinking about either disease or health. A hospital has at least three times as many people working on getting reimbursement from insurance companies than we have chaplains to provide spiritual care!

Fortunately, most of us do not think about all these fragmented systems most of the time. We are not patients; we are fathers, mothers, sisters and brothers, church members, neighbors, employees, students, teachers, volunteers in a zillion settings, and, almost always, shoppers. And sometimes we just walk the dog around the block.

It helps to think of the *whole* system as alive. The people of Lesotho with their concept of *Bophelo* have it right: the lives of any of us depend on the life of the whole. There is no such thing as parts at all. All of these things we separate in our minds are merely facets of one integral thing. It helps in highly practical ways to distinguish between something that is alive and something that is not.

The plethora of roles, organizations, and services are not best understood as things that might go wrong—"risk vectors"—in the language of public health. They are relationships that *usually* go more or less right, especially when they are connected, share some sense of coherent meaning, and act appropriately with a sense of their role toward the very young and old. We need to use language to talk about community that fits a living system because the way you improve the functioning of a living system is to enhance its life qualities—its connectedness, its coherence, its capacity for action (agency), its flow of blessings, and its hopefulness. It's alive.

> **We need to use language to talk about community that fits a living system because the way you improve the functioning of a living system is to enhance its life qualities—its connectedness, its coherence, its capacity for action (agency), its flow of blessings, and its hopefulness. It's alive.**

Cerner is focused on how information flows among its various partners so that the system as a whole can work with less fear, friction, and disconnection. This is really critical but drags every one of the linked structures into the complexities of human relationships including such intangibles as trust and compassion. Living systems keep getting more complicated all the time.

The hospital is losing its walls brick by brick. Services that once *had* to be inside are now more efficiently made available in smaller neighborhood settings. Science and the Leading Causes of Life tell us that the factors that determine our ability to treat someone effectively are largely what has happened in his or her life before coming near us. This means that we are increasingly immersed into the community and its complex webs of trust and choice. This is hard learning for hospitals, to say the least. But we know that the only way to find our institutional life is to seek it among the connections of the whole community system. This isn't symbolic language—it is where our money comes and goes, our employees come and go, as well as all the stuff that matters to us.

We've been talking about mapping the flow of information. Information is only one kind of energy flowing around the system.

Money flows here and there, but so do other kinds of assets including voluntary time and political capital. Every part of the system works much better when its relationships to the other parts of the system work better. This makes for more efficiency and effectiveness, but also for much more intelligence that can drive another lap of innovation. A community that is well connected is capable of responding to new situations with innovative strategies based on shared knowledge and trust. Sounds like life, doesn't it?

A community that is well connected is capable of responding to new situations with innovative strategies based on shared knowledge and trust. Sounds like life, doesn't it?

Fear scatters our energies as it teases us into frittering away our time doing things relevant only to threats. Life concentrates our energies and makes us more effective. Unlike fear, which flits from one distraction to the next, life is multi-relevant, building strengths that apply to multiple phenomena. It focuses our attention on making choices that actually lead to life.

The health care field is filled with cruel tradeoffs and difficult choices involving the basic question of who gets what, when. It is tough enough in a city like Memphis that is surrounded by a sea of poor people. It is much tougher when we start to live into the connections that cross comfortable borders into the interlinked global web of life.

Fear scatters our energies as it teases us into frittering away our time doing things relevant only to threats. Life concentrates our energies and makes us more effective. It focuses our attention on making choices that actually lead to life.

We live in an age of chronic diseases that travel with us over the course of our lives. Although we know we must learn to live with them, we long for a cure, a fix, an escape from whatever afflicts us. Sometimes this actually happens.

169

The balloon in my heart opened up the artery, blood began to flow again, and life returned just as it did when half a century ago I took my first shots of insulin.

But in neither case was there a cure. I left the hospital with diabetes and with an understanding that taking care of my heart would be a life-long exercise. The intersection of the healthcare community with the lives of human beings is both brief and expensive. A single blood test yields a diagnosis of diabetes with which the patient will have to live on an hourly basis for the rest of his or her life. A single MRI determines the presence of cancer. It is not at the clinic or hospital that healing actually takes place. It is within the church, within the neighborhood, within the workplace, and within the family that we live out the consequences of our diagnoses. Each is part of the geography of healing. Each has the opportunity, indeed the responsibility, to speak the language of life. We simply must find and then fearlessly name the causes of life that bring about healing wherever they may be.

One day, before an eye surgery, the anesthesiologists and I were chatting; and I mentioned I was at work on the Geography of Healing.

"You know," he said to me before sending the anesthesia through me, "we really don't fix much here. Once in a while we do, but for the most part we just find what's wrong and patch it up."

"Right," I said. "We must pay attention to the places people actually heal."

After returning from Interfaith Health Program training, our Montana team wondered what we could do to address the healthcare disparities that afflicted our state. In the end we decided we needed to find ways to help churches realize they actually are arenas of healing, and to help hospitals view churches not through the lens of public relations but as genuine partners in healing. Throughout history, churches have cared for members whose lives are changed by strokes, who face cancer, and who live in the shadow of despair. Churches know about healing.

At St. Vincent's Hospital in Billings, Montana, on the first Friday of each month, we decided to bring the healers together. We invited clergy, lay persons, and medical staff to share their experiences working with the mentally ill, setting up parish nursing programs, how one goes about the task of intervention, the art of ministry during the closing chapters of life. The thrilling conversations recognized that healing is not the territory of the hospital, or the clinic, or the church alone. Instead, it is common ground whose partnerships have lain fallow for too long a time.

There is indeed a geography of healing whose landscape we cross over the course of our lives. Along the way we connect with others, we heal, we travel, we nurture the gift of hope, and we find the journey to be a blessing.

Larry

—⁓—

As I was finishing this book, I attended a meeting sponsored by the World Health Organization which was trying to figure out how it should behave in a world of extreme disparity between the lives of those living with AIDS in Africa and those living with AIDS in the rich countries of Europe and North America.[94] How do the Leading Causes of Life help us behave as decent human beings in the context of AIDS? Being decent seems like an appallingly low standard for grown-ups to aim, surely we can do *that*! But being decent focuses on the connections between those in a position to care and those in a position of receiving care. Decency is defined

It is not at the clinic or hospital that healing actually takes place. It is within the church, within the neighborhood, within the workplace, and within the family that we live out the consequences of our diagnoses. Each is part of the geography of healing. Each has the opportunity, indeed the responsibility, to speak the language of life.

by the way that our lives contribute, enable, and nurture the lives of those in the social web at a community scale. Decency is a quality of life.

As this was written, we read of barbaric negotiations concerning whether 2,100 or 1,100 daily calories is a decent level of nutrition to provide the desperate Darfur victims, while at the same time, our politicians pump unfathomable billions of dollars into military expenditures. Even *reading* about this discussion seems indecent. Similar calculation is common in conferences about the "AIDS Orphans" or those living with AIDS. How can we push beyond animal-level indicators of survival and move toward a human quality of decency that begins with an assumption of what is necessary for human life to flourish? "Decency" rests within a causal logic of life. Any less diminishes the lives of all involved in dynamic caring relationships.

Public health workers insist that decent care can be delivered only in the context of broader community. Paul Farmer is an iconic leader of our time equipped with an MD, a Ph.D., and global experience as a physician at Harvard, in Haiti, and a long list of unpronounceable places. He links justice and human rights to community-scale health care.[95] Since the dawn of the modern public health movement in the mid-1800's, such powerful, if minority, voices have located the determinants of health amid social relationships. But even at its best, public health models, as well as the traditional, individual-based, bio-medical model have focused primarily on pathology, diagnosis, and preventing death. Given the limited resources and the expense of sophisticated care and complicated pharmaceuticals, this paradigm invariably contributes to hopelessness in addressing the pandemic of HIV/AIDS in most countries. Public health people, like Farmer, argue that the delivery of decent care to people with HIV/AIDS requires that public-private partnerships make specific services and interventions available to the poorest regions. Such "transfers of wealth" are necessary to break the cycle of poverty, disease, and disparity exemplified in structural violence.[96] Decency demands that we beat back death and its determinants everywhere, aiming at reaching the same standards whether you are trying to be decent in Boston or the mountains of Haiti. Inevitably, we end up in a squabble over how much of this or that service is possible, how big the pile of pills must be in order for us to feel decent enough to achieve some minimal peace of mind. When faced with large and intractable pathologies, it is not surprising that decency seems a standard beyond reach, if not imagination.

Jim Cochrane, one of the initiators of ARHAP, reflects that, "Public health is generally about creating the conditions of health, and not just about immunizations, antibiotics, antiretrovirals, and similar clinical interventions, however important these may be. Public health, in this sense, is long term and not quick fix in its view, social and not merely physiological in its scale, transformative and not just curative in its ambition."[97]

The more you feel like you are negotiating with death all the time, the more you forget about life. You quite literally lose your life: you misplace it and forget where it came from.

The persons who live on the bleeding edge of these terrible discussions about how much death to fight end up dying themselves—argument by argument, pitiful compromise by banal negotiation. Small church clergy in rural Mississippi feel about the same way. Whether you are in Haiti or Hattiesburg, the more you feel like you are negotiating with death all the time, the more you forget about life. You quite literally lose your life: you misplace it and forget where it came from.

Why not look at what causes life, not death? When you think about the implications of all the deadly risks faced by people living with HIV/AIDS in poverty, you'd quickly notice that most of them should not logically be alive and should abdicate any hope for survival. The standard models cannot account for the lives of those made vulnerable by AIDS, especially the children. The landscape for these children is marked by the lack of parents, the lack of a home, the lack of resources, and an incredible vulnerability to the ravages of a hostile world—all made incalculably more toxic by the stigma attached to their situation. AIDS orphans are more likely to be abused and malnourished as are their sick moms and dads. If you add the factors of escalating depression and despair from these variables to the mix, you march steadily toward suffering and death of spirit, mind, and body.

However, many vulnerable children not only survive, but also thrive. What are the threads of vibrancy, vitality, and Leading Causes of Life for these affected children? A "decent" relationship between those of us in a position to care and any one or any million of these children begins by focusing on the causes of life that are working in the kids, in the adults living with AIDS, and, at the very time, in those of us who are finding our lives in relationship to them. We find our life just when we thought it was misplaced forever.

The Leading Causes of Life nurture life where science and rationality dictate there should be none. It is helpful to see that life is present in every community, even before any external analysis or intervention. Thus neither the World Health Organization nor any North American congregation is *beginning* the process of life. They have a more humble role, simply to be a decent partner in nurturing the life that is already there. Our more humble role helps us notice the social structures are alive themselves—not just autonomous recipient individuals. The assets are alive and thus capable of a partnership fit for living things. Decency, in short, is a quality of living human relationships, including those engagements that emerge between those trying to care and those needing care.

> A decent relationship between caregiver and recipient reflects all of the five Leading Causes of Life: connectivity or the feeling of unity with the universe, coherence or meaning, agency or action, blessing or grace, and hope that is an informed vision of the future.

A decent relationship between caregiver and recipient reflects all of the five Leading Causes of Life: connectivity or the feeling of unity with the universe, coherence or meaning, agency or action, blessing or grace, and hope that is an informed vision of the future. Framing the world of a vulnerable child within the logic of these five Leading Causes of Life makes it possible to see life vectors.

We begin in the most concrete place. Our connections to where the stuff of life flows among and through the human relationships where AIDS orphans are. We pay attention to where they experience touch, caring, welcoming, and feeding of body, mind, and spirit. Frequently that connection is some expression of a faith community that includes the child in its extended family. When this connection is alive, a child's immune system responses cascade toward life and health. The most tenuous connection can be a source of increasing life if nurtured and respected as the vital seed that it is.

Not all connections are life giving, however, as anyone stigmatized and alienated by AIDS or poverty can witness. Connection already exists between the most remote African village and any village in the North, but most of these connections are invisible, especially to those on the rich side of the link. Decency demands that we discover the ways in which we are already connected, including those connections that have been damaging. Cotton fields surround Memphis for miles in every direction. These fields, largely owned and farmed by large corporations, receive heavy subsidies from the U.S. government that make it extremely difficult for small farmers in Africa to make a decent living. The connection between Memphis and Africa has a malevolent side. Ignorance serves our interest while occasional acts of charity distract us from the actual connection we share that links wealth to poverty and poverty to AIDS. Decency doesn't end with negotiations over the level of pharmaceuticals available in Zambia. It only ends when all of our connections contribute to the life of the whole. The pills will be easy once we breathe life into our connections.

Coherence can be tricky for a motherless and fatherless child, but even small children are phenomenally good at finding the positive meaning in tragedy and crafting good from it. Every village has a story of an AIDS orphan who survives, thrives, grows to adulthood, masters a caregiving skill, and stays to care for others. While religious TV folk blather superficially about good works, children and parents find good works—in true coherence in the context of caring relationships that honor the realities of their pain and separation.

Decency calls us to be accountable to the shared meaning found among Christians living with AIDS. A poster printed by the Methodist Church of Southern Africa hangs in my office in Memphis that says, "The Church has AIDS." It has hung over my desk for a year, and not a soul here has ever commented on it. This tells me that people can't quite figure out what it means to *their* lives and *their* church. "Are you saying we have AIDS?" They have no problem talking about the picture of the waterfall a few feet away, but to think that *their* church has AIDS—that brings silence.

What does it mean that the mines of South Africa and vast plantations elsewhere in southern Africa created a situation where millions of broken families created a perfect environment for AIDS to flourish? How do we find *Bophelo* or wholeness in such a history? I once met with a powerful foundation executive who challenged me, "Gary, when are you white liberals going to understand that the AIDS crisis in Africa is all about penises being in the wrong places?"

I'm not sure he had noticed that most penises are connected to human beings, which are pretty complicated things. Oversimplification feeds the despair in which AIDS exults. Coherence sees the whole system and all the determinants. Coherence begins with reality and allows us to adapt. It expects to find life where others only find fear and death. Coherence begins with grace and is never surprised by its power to nurture new possibilities.

Life acts, chooses, moves, and *does*. Agency, or "the capacity to do" can seem too much to ask of a vulnerable child, but every village knows that the child who can rise above grief and loss to value his or her own breath of life can become a most powerful agent in his or her environment. Faith communities with limited resources function like extended families and provide multiple opportunities for children to reciprocate caregiving in terms of nurturing younger children or helping with domestic tasks.

> Coherence sees the whole system and all the determinants. Coherence begins with reality and allows us to adapt. It expects to find life where others only find fear and death. Coherence begins with grace and is never surprised by its power to nurture new possibilities.

Agency focuses our attention not just on what others can do, but also on what we can do in our connections. Thousands of congregations and schools have developed a foreign policy in recent years by getting directly involved in a relationship. Agency expects movement, choice, and action. Remember John McKnight's warning about disabling the agency of the recipients of charity? Decency expects agency to be alive among everyone in the system.[98] We now live in such a highly connected world that agency is available to a very large number of entities, mobilized by quick communication, cheap travel, increasingly shared language, and shared meanings. Not all these are entirely helpful; some are actively toxic. The challenge is not the lack of agency, but whether the agency is coherent and life-giving to the connections, a true blessing, and whether it opens a hope that is truly transformational.

Blessing is a bittersweet issue for orphans. But the African model of ancestral ties is potent here. Orphan logic contends that, "I have no parents on this earthly fold, but I am still one of a long line of ancestors." That connectedness to generations past or to come can foster a deep desire to "bless" or "make my parents proud," and "keep the line going."

Decent blessing forces us to think of the future, not only of our sub-tribe (my Norwegian-American branch lost in the South), but also of the whole human web. Blessing lifts the horizon of action beyond the immediate provision of charitable goods and services to look at the trajectory of the entire relationship. Dr. King talked about the long arc of history bending toward justice. Blessing helps us see the curvature of our own lifetimes.

Hope is crucial for those most vulnerable; but hope is also most telling for those in a position to care. Decent hope is hope for the whole, not just this child or that village, this month or next. Chronically ill patients know that it is not medications or surgeries that help us all get up in the morning—it's simply hope. Hope that things will get better, that I won't go hungry today, that the sun will shine, that the pain will stop, that love will overcome evil and injustice. Older children frequently live on the hope for their younger siblings. So, too, does hope infuse the whole connected entity. Is it possible to seek a hope that includes African villages *and* Memphis? If not, it is unlikely that we will find a common future in which to live.

The expression of agency by those who care contributes to their own lives, just as it may extend a vital effect to those receiving their care. We see this vividly in the lives of our 10,000 workers of

Methodist Le Bonheur Healthcare where we are trying to be decent amid a predictable pattern of disease and injury rooted in poverty and disparity. Decency, in our context, is not limited to our attempt to provide an equitable standard of services to every one of the 3,000 patients we see daily. Rather, decency means participating in their lives in a way that fully appreciates their life connections, their expressions of meaning, their continued agency in their family and neighbors, their role as a source of blessing on their connections, and as people who hope for themselves and those things that will last after them. Our staff members who enter into a healing relationship with our patients report much greater job satisfaction, tend to stay with us, and express pride in their work. They are, in short, made more alive by the way they contribute to the causes of life of our patients.

> **Rather, decency means participating in their lives in a way that fully appreciates their life connections, their expressions of meaning, their continued agency in their family and neighbors, their role as a source of blessing on their connections, and as people who hope for themselves and those things that will last after them.**

By focusing on the living assets present in the social structures of those needing care, we come into a decent relationship with them, so both of us are more alive. The first step toward decency is to enter into a living relationship that nurtures the connections, coherence, agency, blessing, and hope that are already present. Decency looks for one of the five Leading Causes of Life and begins to nurture it. Decency begins with the life that is and builds on it, rather than focusing on (and, in the process, magnifying) the all-too-obvious gaps. For instance, one might focus on the powerful connections that exist among the children rather than their shattered bond with dying parents or a stigmatizing village.

Decency recognizes that in many cases death wins. But it notices that in many cases it does not. In even the most difficult situations, life is also happening—always trying to cause more life. A decent relationship with those needing care is to nurture their life even as

178

we try to beat back death. It is the least we can do and remain human ourselves.

Caregivers find their life in the relationship with those receiving care. Justice seekers do the same. Leaders find their life in the life of their networks, participating in the vital processes that cause the life of the whole. That is the way of life.

—⁓—

One of the ironies of our time is that many people who serve in caring professions experience poor health. Perhaps

The first step toward decency is to enter into a living relationship that nurtures the connections, coherence, agency, blessing, and hope that are already present. Decency looks for one of the five Leading Causes of Life and begins to nurture it. Decency begins with the life that is and builds on it, rather than focusing on the all-too-obvious gaps.

the most ironic of all is the strikingly below average health of clergy. Age for age, clergy have significantly greater incidences of chronic disease, heart and GI tract conditions, and stress, which is a bit embarrassing for a group preaching about life every week. Clergy today have, on average, a pattern of health that is significantly worse than the average American.[99] There is something about the role of clergy that either attracts people prone to illness or people who find the role to be highly stressful once they get into it. To a large extent, this is visible in other caring roles including teachers, nurses, physicians, and those who care for the community. But, there is something especially ironic about the clergy that is particularly painful to me.

When we meet with clergy about their health, we talk about their Leading Causes of Life. It usually takes about an hour for them to quit talking about the life of their congregation and community and gradually turn toward their own lives. When the clergy come to our hospital for a couple days and are confronted with their health indicators by means of a thorough physical and "behavioral risk assessment," they aren't surprised. Even the times when they learn of some specific disease condition they have, they aren't really shocked. Then we spend the time on Leading Causes of Life, and they *are* surprised to learn that there is a way to talk about their *life*, not just their various body parts.

At the global, local, and personal scale, health reflects life, not just death. "The way people seek health is profoundly symptomatic of what they make of life and what life is making of them," said David Jenkins a quarter century ago.[100] He was reflecting on what the church should be doing to advance health across the world. But he could have been talking to a handful of pastors in Mississippi just as well.

The Lilly Endowment shares this interest in clergy health because they have invested hundreds of millions of dollars to support theological education, clergy training, and congregational studies.[101] Gradually, it has become obvious that the clergy are, meanwhile, becoming less and less healthy. This is a large-scale pattern that is profoundly ironic: clergy as a group tend toward ill health, despite the fact they are called to promote life. How can that be?

As always, the first right thing to do is to get the question framed correctly: in this case, the question is about the well-lived life of clergy, not just their physical or even mental disease indicators. What do we need for a well-lived life? The working group on the subject came up with a list of components that any such life would include like deep and regular access to the nourishment of the Spirit: Scripture, prayer, liturgy, retreat, study, worship, sacraments, and the other living gifts of tradition.[102] But pastors also need to be members in, as Craig Dykstra and John Wimmer of The Lilly Endowment call it, a "community of competent shared practice." Every word of this phrase ignites a powerful question. Few clergy feel themselves in a *community*, many doubt their training prepares them with relevant *competence*, and they feel this competence is rarely shared in *practice*.

Dykstra and Wimmer note that pastors need not just one, but at least four kinds of communities that make for a well-lived *pastoral* life, including a community of other pastors who share competence in this work, and also a congregation where one is part of a community practicing a Christian Way of Life. Pastors need to be part of a family that shares life, joys, sorrows, and leisure. Pastors need to feel like they are members of the larger, public world. Pastors need some degree of freedom to improvise in order to make a difference. This depends on training, education, openness to the idea of innovating, and a decent and functional institutional setting in which to work. Pastors, like anyone, need resources for health—physical and mental—including proper diet, exercise, and access to good medical care. Pastors also need the material goods necessary for a well-lived pastoral life such as income, education, travel, a home, and access to beauty.

Almost any caring professional needs pretty much the same kinds of things to live their lives of service well. Just like AIDS orphans, the list of stuff and relationships is quite long because the length of a well-lived life is much longer. People are in our hospitals for an average of about five days per event in a lifetime that in the United States extends an average of almost 80 years.[103] When you stop focusing on the occasional disease event, the horizon expands and gets more complicated. Then, the question shifts away from the long list of required things for healing to the process that creates all the stuff for living. That's where the Leading Causes of Life begin to be really helpful. Stuff comes from life; life does not come from stuff. Even when you know your own prospects for a well-lived life will, over its course, end up using a lot of stuff, it is more helpful to focus on life.

Things *do* flow across our vital connections, but the connections are there first. And the connections are sustained—sometimes initiated—by rich threads of meaning. The connections offer up opportunities to support one's own agency, but can also stifle it. So you might need to choose to move away from connections that are no longer life-giving. As a human being who is alive, you can do that. Frequently, the connections that matter most have a longer life span than our own—denominations, cities, families, and neighborhoods all precede us and will, usually, continue after us. So the connections can be the trellis on which the webs of blessing grow. They are where we both receive and give the stuff of life. Sometimes, the connections can be quite the opposite, of course. For clergy, the connectional systems that were designed to foster their life and denominations have adapted poorly into the changed environment of the 21st century. Doctors, nurses, and teachers say the same thing.

In our current era, the connections that were once life-giving are now life-inhibiting. Those connections must adapt for us to thrive in the new circumstance. Fortunately, Salk would remind us, those connections are not hard-wired into our DNA. We can—because we are alive—change. The connections can be a place to look for life, to reverse the flow.

Many of us born in the mid-twentieth century were bred to think of life in a way that is no longer likely (a job with a guaranteed pension), or interesting (one job for our whole career), or productive (defined by measures that now seem uninspiring). Those life expectations turn out to be not only impossible, but also unattractive. Life looks like something different. But what? The Leading Causes of Life help us imagine our lives well-lived because they help us know where to look.

—⁀꙰⁀—

Closing Thoughts: Life About Life

Anybody can make a list of what's wrong in Africa, Memphis, Kansas, or pretty much any place in the world. Most of us have a long list of what's wrong in our own lives, for that matter. Any of your friends can tell you what is wrong with you, in case you're having trouble remembering. Adding to these lists is a waste of time for it tells us little about where to go.

> **The whole point of this book is that it is possible to live a life that is about life.**

It takes a mind tuned to life to see the life of a community. It takes life to see life. It takes life to see the life clearly enough to love it, respect it, and intelligently hope for it so you can serve it.

The whole point of this book is that it is possible to live a life that is about life—your own and the persons and neighborhoods and planet that is home to all that matters. That's all that any grown-up hopes for.

It is not delusional to seek life.

For there will come a day when you will lay all that you have down and hand all that you love to another to tend it. On that day, nobody will talk about the great problems you fought. They will talk about your life and the life it made possible in those you loved, in the connections that live after you.

It is amazing how the closing thoughts of a book draw us to our beginnings. On the wall, beside the piano in my childhood home, my mother kept a framed poem called "Play It Again." I do not know who wrote it, but its phrases left an indelible impact. I remember it first says to play the piece, and find the melody. The next lines build on the first. It says then play it again to hear the harmony. Play it again, this time to feel the rhythm. And play it again to understand its flow. Play it again, this time slowly. And play it again, putting it all together. Then, at the end, the poem lovingly and gently says to then, "Play it again."

Life sets music before us and asks us to practice the art of connection that forms hymns and symphonies. It asks us to practice hope and to practice blessing. Then it asks us, over and over again, to "Play it again."

Every practice session can't help but bring us closer to life itself and gives us the power to bring about change. Each session leads me to a million "What ifs?" Why shouldn't discharge from a hospital include a caring conversation about hope? Why aren't there pages written for the patient's family and friends that recognize the healing power of connection? Why don't church choirs practice for Sunday by walking down a hospital corridors singing, *"There are angels hovering round,"* and the hymn of the week as part of their ministry of music? What happens when churches recognize they are the healing arenas in which we live out the diagnoses of our lives? Each session makes me wonder how the discordant notes of a 9/11, or a sour meeting, or a lost relationship will find resolution when we take time to practice, practice, and then practice again the elemental notes of life. They make me wonder how tonight's meeting of the board at Joliet Christian Church (Disciples of Christ) can best be given over to the question, "How can we best bless and connect with life in this town?" They make me wonder how we best work *with* the grain of life instead of *against* it. As much as they animate my imagination about the future, they bring me into a deeper appreciation of the present as well.

It had been almost four years since I had seen Jared, who I wrote about in Chapter 4. His life moved on since his confirmation, and we had to move away from Big Timber for the months of rehabilitation. I had told him that one day or another his paper would surface in a book, and that I'd let him know when that happened. A week before our editing of this book came to an end I decided to pay a visit to the cafeteria/kitchen at Sweet Grass County High School in Big Timber, Montana, where Jared's mother, Anita, works. I walked into the kitchen, and sure enough Anita was there. So were Jane, Linda, and Helen, all visiting together while preparing the food.

"Anita, guess what?" I said. "Jared's going to be in the book. He's in the chapter we've written about coherence. Who could ever forget that paper."

Tears began to form in Anita's eyes. "I've still got it," she said.

Jane remembered the day Jared shared his paper and so did the others who had heard about the day a 14-year-old shared the truth of his life, his hope, and his faith.

"How's he doing?"

"Good! He's back in school at Montana State University."

"Will you tell him his paper is in the book? And tell him he owes me a fishing trip."

"I will," she said.

And then the conversation among friends drifted from the harbor of coherence to the ocean of connection. When we learned a relationship had blossomed we offered our congratulations, a bevy of teases, entertained a few blushes, and shared the sublime feeling of goodwill. We wondered how the other confirmands were doing. I said I had to check up on them, to reconnect with them. Then it was time to get the rolls in the oven, and our conversation drew to a close. It had been sweet enough, and deep enough, and compelling enough to call it a blessing.

Let us sound out life's melody; and then play it again.

Let us trace its harmony. And then play it again.

Let us hear its rhythm. And then play it again.

And then, together, let us play it again.

Jared is in the book.

And so are you.

Larry

—◇—

Many would recognize this as the benediction, a sending-forth. And so do we.

We want our lives to be about life.

We want to be with people who are working on life and build connections that help us help each other do that year after year until we hand our work over to others. We want to hear songs and Scripture that hold up powerful meanings against the silly and distracted clutter of our public discourse. We want to talk in plain language about the life among us, so that we can laugh, cry, and pray at the right time. We want to make the choices and take the risks that make possible the next generation. We want to think about those who have come before us and those coming along behind us, so that we can feel like worthy participants in the web that connects us all.

That's what life wants us to do. Indeed, it causes us to want those things. The very desire for life is testimony that it is already in us and among us saying yes.

ENDNOTES

[1] Jonas Salk, **Survival of the Wisest** (Harper & Row, 1973).

[2] Aaron Antonovsky, **Unraveling the Mystery of Health: How People Manage Stress and Stay Well** (Jossey Bass Inc., 1987).

[3] John Wesley, **Primitive Remedies** (Woodbridge Press, 1973).

[4] W. S. Hudson, ed., **Sources of American Spirituality**, *Walter Rauschenbusch: Selected Writings* (Paulist Press, 1984).

[5] Salk, **Survival of the Wisest**.

[6] William Foege, "Foreword: On Values & Vulnerability, the Value of Religious Health Assets," in **Strong Partners: Realigning Religious Health Assets for Community Health** (The Carter Center, 1997); pp. 2–4.

[7] National Center for Health Statistics, "Life expectancy by age by race and sex, 1900–2003, **U.S. Life Tables, 2003, Table 11**" (Center for Disease Control); http://www.cdc.gov/nchs/fastats/lifexpec.htm.

[8] Gary R. Gunderson, "Introduction: On the Full Menu of Assets, the Faith Health Community Confluence" in **Strong Partners: Realigning Religious Health Assets for Community Health** (The Carter Center, 1997); pp. 6–10.

[9] National Center for Health Statistics, **U.S. Life Tables, 2003, Table 11**.

[10] Michael Crichton, Maria Scotch Marmo, David Koepp and Crichton, *Jurassic Park*, script adapted from novel by Michael Crichton, **Jurassic Park**, 1994.

[11] "Chronic Diseases: The Leading Causes of Death in Montana" from http://www.cdc.gov/nccdphp/states/index.htm.

[12] National Council of Churches, **The Yearbook of American and Canadian Churches, 2006 Edition**.

[13] Marshall Kreuter, Christopher DeRosa, Elizabeth Howze, and Grant Baldwin, "Understanding Wicked Problems: A Key to Advancing Environmental Health Promotion," **Health Education & Behavior**, Vol. 31, No. 4 (2004); pp. 441–454.

[14] Salk, **Survival of the Wisest**.

[15] Ibid.

[16] Desmond Tutu, **No Future Without Forgiveness** (Doubleday, 1999).

[17] http://en.wikipedia.org/Miasma_theory_of_disease.

[18] T.N.K. Raju, "Ignac Semmelweis and the Etiology of Fetal and Neonatal Sepsis," **Journal of Perinatology**, June 1999; Vol. 19, No. 4; pp. 307–310.

[19] National Center for Health Statistics, **U.S. Life Tables, 2003, Table 11**.

[20] Robert N. Anderson and Betty L. Smith, "Deaths: Leading Causes for 2002, **National Vital Statistics Reports**," Vol. 53, No. 17, March 7, 2005.

[21] Salk, **Survival of the Wisest**.

[22] Gary R. Gunderson, "On Faith, Science & Hope: Linking Faith and Science," in **Strong Partners: Realigning Religious Health Assets for Community Health** (The Carter Center, 1997); pp. 12–21.

[23] Gary R. Gunderson, **Deeply Woven Roots** (Fortress Press, 1997).

[24] Salk, **Survival of the Wisest.**

[25] Antonovsky, **Unraveling the Mystery of Health.**

[26] Ibid; p. xi.

[27] Tom Munnecke, **Ensembles and Transformations** (Science Applications International Corporation, 2000).

[28] www.habitat.org.

[29] These questions led to the formation of the American Board of Commissioners for Foreign Mission of the Congregational Church, now part of the United Church of Christ.

[30] E. Eger, S.R. Schweinberger, R.J. Dolan, and R.N. Henson, "Familiarity Enhances Invariance of Face Representations in Human Ventral Visual Cortex: fMRI Evidence," **Neuroimage**, Vol. 26, No. 4, July 15, 2005; pp. 1128–1139.

[31] Gregory L. Fricchione, "Separation, Attachment, and Altruistic Love: The Evolutionary Basis for Medical Caring," in **Altruism and Altruistic Love**, edited by Stephen G. Post, Lynn G. Underwood, Jeffery P. Schloss, William B. Hurlbut (Oxford University Press, 2002).

[32] Fricchione, "Religious Issues in the Context of Medical Illness," in **Psychiatric Care of the Medical Patient**, second edition edited by Alan Stoudemire, Barry S. Fogel, Donna B. Greenburg (Oxford University Press, 2000).

[33] Gary R. Gunderson, **Boundary Leaders** (Fortress Press, 2004).

[34] Ibid.

[35] Gunderson, **Deeply Woven Roots.**

[36] U.S. Census Bureau, **Current Population Survey, March Supplements: 1970–2000.**

[37] Jill Oliver, Lauren Graham, Barbara Schmid, **ARHAP Literature Review: Sub-Saharan Africa** (ARHAP, 2006).

[38] Jill Oliver, Lauren Graham, Barbara Schmid, **ARHAP Bibliography: Focus on Africa: Working at the Intersection of Religion and Public Health: A Bounded Field of Unknowing** (ARHAP, 2006).

[39] http://st.wiktionary.org/wiki/bophelo.

[40] Paul Germond, Lauren Graham, and Sepetla Molapo, **ARHAP International Colloquium**, Willow Park, Gauteng, South Africa, 2005; p. 69.

[41] Frank Durabont, *The Shawshank Redemption*, movie script adapted from novella by Stephen King, **Rita Hayworth and Shawshank Redemption**, 1994.

[42] Viktor E. Frankl, **Man's Search for Meaning** (Washington Square Press/Pocket Books, 1985).

[43] Antonovsky, **Unraveling the Mystery of Health**.

[44] Viktor E. Frankl, **... trotzdem Ja zum Leben sagen. Ein Psychologe erlebt das Konzentrationslager** (Kösel-Verlag Gmbh + Co., 1977).

[45] Fred Douglas Smith Jr., "Without a Vision: A Prophetic Christian Religious Education for Black Boys" (Emory University, Division of Religion, 1996).

[46] John Wilcher and Joe Ranager, "A Descriptive Analysis of Pastors Clinic Data at Methodist Hospital," presentation at clergy health conference, Nov. 2003, Church Health Center.

[47] Antonovsky, **Unraveling the Mystery of Health**.

[48] Charles Marsh, **Beloved Community: How Faith Shapes Social Justice From the Civil Rights Movement to Today** (Basic Books, 2005).

[49] www.alban.org.

[50] www.louisville-institute.org/secondary/pastoralgrants.asp.

[51] Steve DeGruchy, "Assets and Agency" in Papers and Proceedings of the African Religious Health Assets Programme International Colloquium, James Cochrane and Barbara Schmid, eds., Pietermarizburg, R. (University of Capetown, South Africa: August 2003).

[52] Ibid.

[53] Oliver, Graham, Schmid, **ARHAP Literature Review.**

[54] Liz Thomas, Barbara Schmid, Malibongwe Gwele, Rosemond Ngubo, James R. Cochrane, **"Let Us Embrace": The Role and Significance of an Integrated Faith-Based Initiative for HIV and AIDS**. Africa Religious Health Assets Programme (ARHAP) Research Report: Masangane Case Study (Eastern Cape, South Africa, 2006).

[55] Ibid.

[56] John McKnight, **Careless Societies: Community and Its Counterfeit** (Basic Books, 1996).

[57] Ibid.

[58] National Center for Health Statistics, **U.S. Life Tables, 2003, Table 11**.

[59] Marty Haugen, **"Turn My Heart: A Sacred Journey From Brokenness to Healing"** (G.I.A. Publications, Inc., 2003). Compact Disc available at www.giamusic.com.

[60] www.talkorigins.org/faqs/homs/species.html.

[61] Salk, **Survival of the Wisest**.

[62] Gunderson, **Boundary Leaders**.

[63] www.one.org.

[64] Fricchione, "Separation, Attachment, and Altruistic Love."

[65] D.H. Ingvar, "Memory of the Future: An Essay on the Temporal Organization of Conscious Awareness," **Human Neurobiology**, Vol. 4; pp. 127–136.

[66] Ronald H. Bainton, **Here I Stand: A Life of Martin Luther** (Penguin Books, 1950).

[67] Emily Dickinson, "Hope is a thing with feathers," in **The Selected Poems of Emily Dickinson** (Little, Brown, and Company, 1924).

[68] Ingvar, "Memory of the Future."

[69] Francis Lappé and Anna Lappé, **Hope's Edge: The Next Diet for a Small Planet** (Jeremy Tarcher, 2003).

[70] Ibid; p. 9.

[71] Garrison Keillor, ed., **Good Poems for Hard Times** (Penguin Group, 2005).

[72] Ibid; p. viii.

[73] Dietrich Bonhoeffer, **Discipleship**. Translated by Barbara Green and Reinhard Krauss (Fortress Press, 2001).

[74] The United Methodist Church, **2004 Statistical Review: The United Methodist Church** (General Council on Finance and Administration, 2005).

[75] See reports from The General Council of Finance and Administration of The United Methodist Church at: http://www.gcfa.org/excel/ConfTablesExcelforWeb-AnnualReport2006.xls and http://www.gcfa.org/excel/Clergy2006EthMem-Gen.xls. See also *2008 Yearbook of American and Canadian Churches* (Abingdon Press, 2008).

[76] Association of Clinicians for the Underserved, Strength for Serving (Virginia: acu@clinicians.org, 2006).

[77] Gary R. Gunderson, **Good News for the Whole Community: Reflections on the History of the First Century of the Social Gospel Movement**, presented as The Earl Lecture at the Pacific School of Religion, January 28, 1999; available at www.ih-pnet.org.

[78] Corey Keyes, **Flourishing: Positive Psychology and the Well-Lived Life** (American Psychological Association, 2003).

[79] Mihaly Csikszentmihalyi, **Flow: The Psychology of Optimal Experience** (Harper Perennial, 1990).

[80] James Pennebaker, **Opening Up: The Healing Power of Confiding in Others** (William Morrow and Company, Inc., 1990).

[81] Dean Ornish, **Love and Survival: The Scientific Basis for the Healing Power of Intimacy** (HarperCollins Publisher, 1998).

[82] Gunderson, **Boundary Leaders**.

[83] Institute of Medicine Division of Health Promotion and Disease Prevention, **Improving Health in the Community** (National Academy Press, 1997).

[84] Steve DeGruchy, Sinatra Matimelo, Debbie Jones, Sepetla Molapo, and Paul Germond, **PIRANHA: Participatory Inquiry Into Religious Health Assets, Networks and Agency, Practitioner's Workbook** (ARHAP, 2005).

[85] http://www.who.int/tdr/diseases/oncho/default.htm.

[86] Deborah McFarland, "When You Come to a Fork in the Road…Take it!" in **ARHAP International Colloquium Papers and Proceedings** (Willow Park, Gautang South Africa, July 2005).

[87] Oliver, Graham, Schmid, **ARHAP Literature Review**.

[88] Thomas, Schmid, Gwele, Ngubo, Cochrane, "**Let Us Embrace.**"

[89] DeGruchy, Matimelo, Jones, Molapo, and Germond, **PIRANHA.**

[90] Oliver, Graham, Schmid, **ARHAP Bibliography**.

[91] Foege, "Foreword: On Values & Vulnerability."

[92] Howard Clinebell, **Ecotherapy: Healing Ourselves, Healing the Earth** (Fortress Press, 1996).

[93] Keyes, **Flourishing: Positive Psychology and the Well-Lived Life**.

[94] Gary R. Gunderson and Teresa F. Cutts, "A Decent Care for Life," in *Restoring Hope: Decent Care in the Midst of HIV/AIDS*, edited by Ted Karpf, J. Todd Ferguson, Robin Swift, and Jeffery V. Lazarus (Palgrave Macmillan, 2008).

[95] Paul Farmer, **Pathologies of Power: Health, Human Rights and the New War on the Poor** (University of California Press, 2003).

[96] D.A. Walton , P.E. Farmer, W. Lambert, F. Leandre, S.P. Koenig, J.S. Mukherjee, "Integrated HIV Prevention and Care Strengthens Primary Health Care: Lessons from Rural Haiti," **Journal of Public Health Policy**, 2004, Vol. 25, No. 2; pp. 137–158.

[97] James Cochrane, "Reconceptualizing Religion and Public Health," **ARHAP International Colloquium Papers and Proceedings** (Willow Park, Gautang South Africa, July 2005); p. 6.

[98] McKnight, **Careless Societies**.

[99] Bob Wells, "**Which Way to Clergy Health?**" reprinted from **Divinity**, Fall 2002; http://www.pulpitandpew.duke.edu/clergyhealth.html.

[100] David Jenkins, **The Quest for Health and Wholeness** (German Institute for Medical Missions, 1981); p. xii.

[101] www.lillyendowment.org/religion_spe.html.

[102] Craig Dykstra and John Wimmer, "Toward Narrating the Well-Lived Pastoral Life," unpublished manuscript (Indianapolis, IN, 2005).

[103] National Center for Health Statistics, **U.S. Life Tables, 2003, Table 11**.

PRAISE FOR *LEADING CAUSES OF LIFE*

"What a refreshing meditation and guide this is! Gary Gunderson and Larry Pray lead us through wonderful stories of hope, imagination, and courage—all of which lead to the regeneration of both community and individual life. In a time when almost all social commentary asks us to contemplate our needs, problems, and deficiencies—the causes of death—this wonderfully readable volume guides us to another powerful set of realities, those which produce life and hope. Anyone who cares about and strives to understand ways to move toward healthy and vital communities will want to keep *Leading Causes of Life* close by."

Dr. Jody Kretzmann
Asset Based Community Development Institute
Northwestern University

"Jesus said he came that all creation might have abundant life. A profound irony threatens this simple truth in our age: because we seek to create lifestyles of abundance chiefly by attempting to postpone death, we may actually miss life itself. Gunderson and Pray have offered us a powerful remedy. For *Leading Causes of Life* is above all about what it takes to create and sustain a way of life that truly gives life. May all who read it learn to look for 'vital signs' around them in new ways, and thereby begin again to foster life abundant for the people, families, institutions, and communities in their reach."

John Wimmer
Program Director, Religion
Lilly Endowment Inc.

"Gunderson and Pray turn our current paradigm of disease and treatment upside down and capture our imaginations and hearts as they offer a new perspective from which to think about practices that lead to health and healing. This book is a 'must-read' for pastors, laity, physicians, and community leaders who want to move from a focus on disease to a focus on life."

Bishop Janice Riggle Huie
The United Methodist Church

Read more at www.leadingcausesoflife.org.